CW00482468

ISBN: 978 1 80282 191 8
Editor: Tim Ripley
Senior editor, specials:
Roger Mortimer
Email: roger.mortimer@
keypublishing.com
Design: SJmagic DESIGN SERVICES, India
Cover design: Dan Hilliard
Head designer: Steve Donovan
Advertising Sales Manager:
Brodie Baxter
Email: brodie.baxter@
keypublishing.com
Tel: 01780 755131
Advertising Production:
Rebecca Antoniades
Email: rebecca.antoniades@
keypublishing.com

Subscription/Mail Order
Key Publishing Ltd, PO Box 300,
Stamford, Lincs, PE9 1NA
Tel: 01780 480404
Fax: 01780 757812
Subscriptions email:
subs@keypublishing.com
Mail Order email:
orders@keypublishing.com
Website: www.keypublishing.com/shop

Publishing
Group CEO: Adrian Cox
Publisher: Mark Elliott
Head of Publishing: Finbarr O'Reilly
Chief Publishing Officer: Jonathan Jackson
Key Publishing Ltd, PO Box 100,
Stamford, Lincs, PE9 1XP
Tel: 01780 755131
Website: www.keypublishing.com

Printing
Precision Colour Printing Ltd, Haldane,
Halesfield 1, Telford, Shropshire. TF7 4QQ

Distribution
Seymour Distribution Ltd,
2 Poultry Avenue, London, EC1A 9PU
Enquiries Line: 02074 294000.
We are unable to guarantee the
bonafides of any of our advertisers.
Readers are strongly recommended
to take their own precautions before
parting with any information or
item of value, including, but not
limited to money, manuscripts,
photographs or personal information
in response to any advertisements
within this publication.

© Key Publishing Ltd 2022
All rights reserved. No part of this
magazine may be reproduced or
transmitted in any form by any
means, electronic or mechanical, including
photocopying, recording or by any
information storage and retrieval
system, without prior permission in
writing from the copyright owner.
Multiple copying of the contents
of the magazine without prior
written approval is not permitted.

CONTENTS

Battle for the Falklands

4 .... Battle for the Falklands
6 .... History of the Falklands
                and Argentina
8 .... Commanding the War
10 .... War on Sea
12 .... War in the Air
14 .... War on Land
16 .... The Nott Review
18 .... The Junta decides to
                Seize Las Malvinas
20 .... Scrap Metal Men Land
                on South Georgia
22 .... *Operation Rosario*
26 .... The Empire Strikes Back
30 .... Fortress Malvinas
32 .... Rejoice, Rejoice
36 .... Into the Total Exclusion Zone
38 .... *Operation Black Buck*
40 .... Harrier Strike
42 .... Sink the *Belgrano*
46 .... Exocet attack on HMS *Sheffield*
50 .... Clearing the Decks for Action
52 .... Pebble Island Raid
54 .... Covert Operations in
                Chile and Argentina
56 .... Forming the Second Wave
58 .... Moving into Position
60 .... D-Day at San Carlos Water
62 .... Frigates vs Skyhawks
66 .... May 25, 1982
68 .... Victory at Goose Green
72 .... On to Mount Kent
74 .... Yomping to Port Stanley
76 .... Chinook Bravo November
78 .... Disaster at Bluff Cove
82 .... General Moore's Battle Plan
84 .... Bombarding Port Stanley
86 .... Mount Longdon
88 .... Twin Sister
90 .... Mount Harriet
92 .... Mount Tumbledown
94 .... Wireless Ridge
96 .... The Argentine Retreat
98 .... White Flags Over Stanley
100 .... Clearing Up the Islands
102 .... The Task Force Returns
104 .... Learning the Lessons
106 .... The Islands and Britain's
                Garrison Today
108 .... Royal Navy Task Force
112 .... British Ground and Air Units
114 .... In Memorial

PHOTO CREDITS
The author has attempted, where possible, to credit
the originators of all the images used in this publication.
Any errors will be corrected in future editions.

Royal Marines advance toward Port Stanley.
(DPL)

The loss of HMS *Sheffield* to an Argentine Exocet missile attack was a major shock to the British armed forces, government and public. *(DPL)*

Argentine navy Super Étendard jets sank one British warship and a cargo vessel. Fortunately, the Argentines only had five of the air launched version of the deadly missile and could not get any more. *(US Navy)*

Once the war was over, the British spent months clearing up abandoned Argentine equipment and mines. Minefields took decades to clear with ordnance still being found in October 2020. *(DPL)*

BATTLE FOR THE FALKLANDS

40 Years On

F orty years ago, Britain and Argentina went to war to control the Falkland Islands, or Islas Malvinas as the Argentines call them. Both nations claim the archipelago that lies some 500 kilometres off the coast of Argentina in the South Atlantic. The dispute escalated into a bloody war that cost just over 900 lives.

Fleets of warships, squadrons of fighter jets and battalions of ground troops were eventually committed by both sides to a struggle that lasted just under three months.

It was one of the first wars of the modern media era, and dramatic footage of burning ships, air raids, anti-aircraft missile barrages and landing craft putting troops ashore on the islands captivated audiences around the world.

For all the wall-to-wall news coverage at the time there was much that was not revealed by the participants. In the intervening 40 years a huge quantity of new information has come to light.

The main commanders and senior officers on both sides have published their memoirs, explaining the complex planning and decision making behind the key events. Scores of veterans have also

The aircraft carrier HMS *Hermes* was the flag ship of the British task group operating around the Falklands. *(DPL)*

Around half of the Falkland Islands 1,800 population in 1982 lived in the capital, Port Stanley. *(GFDL)*

The Type 22 frigate, HMS *Brilliant*, equipped with the Sea Wolf short range air defence missiles received its baptism of fire during the Falklands war. Many lessons were learnt about the effectiveness or otherwise of guided missiles in naval warfare. *(DPL)*

produced accounts of their experiences, adding considerable understating to what happened during those dramatic days.

A great deal of new and previously highly secret information has been made public in a series of British and Argentine official documents. This includes intelligence information that led to the sinking of the cruiser ARA *General Belgrano*, technical disclosures about how HMS *Sheffield*'s defence failed to protect it from a deadly Exocet missile and after-action reports on the effectiveness of British surface-to-air missiles.

Both Argentina and Britain have published official campaign histories and commissions into the conduct of the war. These shed important light on how the war was fought by both senior and junior commanders. Some of this information was highly secret until only a few years ago. These studies revealed for the first time the Argentine battle plans for the invasion of the Malvinas. The lid has

also been lifted on Britain's secret efforts to gather intelligence on Argentine air bases from neutral Chile and plans to mount special forces raids on these strategic facilities.

Hopefully, this publication will pull this new information together to explain how the Battle for the Falklands unfolded and give readers an insight into what those who fought in the conflict experienced. A remarkable collection of photographs from both sides in the war brings this remarkable story to life for readers who are too young to remember the initial media coverage of the conflict.

Over the past 40 years I have had the privilege of meeting many veterans of the conflict. Their insights and experience prompted my continuing interest in the events 1982.

While accounts from some British participants in the Falklands War have a 'Boys Own' adventure feel about them, it is quickly apparent that many veterans were deeply affected and traumatised by their experiences.

At the end of the publication, we pay tribute to the fallen of both sides in the conflict.

A common feeling from many veterans is, 'but for Lady Luck I would have been dead or seriously wounded'. The cruelty of chance was very apparent to me during the spring of 1982 while a student at Lancaster University. Two of my lecturers, Dr Martin Edmonds, and Professor Hugh Tinker, had family members serving with the Royal Navy in the South Atlantic. Both their ships were hit by Argentine bombs or missiles. Fortunately, an Argentine bomb bounced off the deck of HMS *Broadsword* and Lieutenant Commander Graham Edmonds survived the war. Lieutenant David Tinker was not so fortunate and was killed when an Exocet missile hit HMS *Glamorgan* in the final hours of the conflict.

Tim Ripley
Editor
March 2022

Abandoned Argentine helmets after the surrender at Goose Green. *(DPL)*

In the past decade, the Royal Navy has replaced its Falklands era aircraft carriers with the new Queen Elizabeth-class vessels, underlining its belief in the ships being critical to naval warfare. *(DPL)*

In 1982 the Falkland Islands were economically dependent on sheep farming and many Islanders believed the British government had deliberately run down the islands to make it easier to strike a deal with Argentina. *(DPL)*

HISTORY OF THE ISLANDS AND ARGENTINA

The Seeds of War are Sown

European explorers were first recorded as visiting the islands now known as the Falklands in 1690, when the English sea captain John Strong made land fall en route to Chile.

The first recorded settlement was established in 1764 when French colonists founded Port Louis on the island now known as East Falkland. Two years later British colonists established the Port Egmont settlement. The islands then became a venue for imperial rivalry when the French ceded their settlement to Spain, who subsequently sent an expedition to evict the British settlers. But they were allowed to return in 1771 after Madrid and London settled their differences.

Britain abandoned its settlement in 1774 but left a plaque behind restating its claim to the islands. The Spanish colonial administration in what is now Argentina also pulled out its garrison in 1811 at the height of the Napoleonic wars.

In 1816 the newly independent Argentina laid claim to the islands, but its rule was temporarily interrupted by a United States Navy warship in 1831. British forces returned to evict the Argentine administration in 1833 but they left again soon afterwards leaving the islands in the hands of traders and herders.

Britain formally established a Crown Colony in 1840 and, soon after, the first wave of Scottish settlers arrived to establish the permanent settlements that remain to this day.

The territorial dispute with Britain over the control of the islands simmered on for the next 140 years but it was rarely at the heart of relations between London and Buenos Aires. For the first century of its independence from Spain, Argentina was an economic powerhouse. During the second half of the 19th century, it had a higher gross domestic product than the United States. Agriculture and industrial development surged, and British companies and expats were heavily involved in this activity. Italian immigrants headed to the country in huge numbers to contribute to its development.

The Falkland Islands were largely untouched by these events and remained a forgotten colonial outpost, reliant on sheep farming and re-supplying passing British ships. However, the island's importance to the British Empire was highlighted in 1914 and 1939 when Royal Navy warships operating from the islands duelled with German raiders in the South Atlantic.

When Britain decided to withdraw from much of its Empire in the late 1950s, the writing looked to be on the wall for the Falklands. Argentine nationalists saw their moment and began a diplomatic campaign to secure the control of the islands. And, in 1966 they succeeded in

The Falkland Islands played a key part in both World War One and Two, acting as a base for the Royal Navy to hunt down and destroy German raiders in the South Atlantic. *(William Lionel Wyllie)*

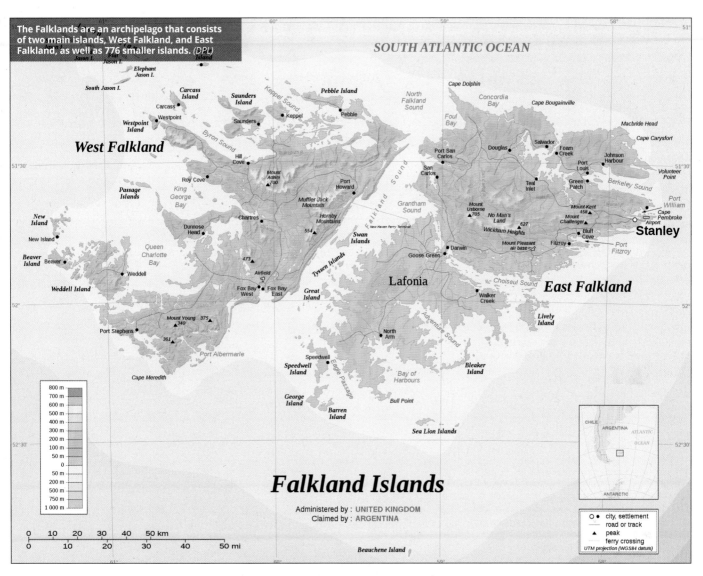

The Falklands are an archipelago that consists of two main islands, West Falkland, and East Falkland, as well as 776 smaller islands. *(DPL)*

SOUTH ATLANTIC OCEAN

West Falkland

East Falkland

Lafonia

Stanley

Falkland Islands

Administered by : UNITED KINGDOM
Claimed by : ARGENTINA

800 m	
700 m	
600 m	
500 m	
400 m	
300 m	
200 m	
100 m	
50 m	
0	
50 m	
200 m	
500 m	
750 m	
1 000 m	

○● city, settlement
— road or track
▲ peak
ferry crossing
UTM projection (WGS84 datum)

getting the United Nations to classify the dispute with Britain as an issue of decolonisation.

The British government had little interest in hanging on to the Falklands or even spending any money on them. Trade and economic links to the booming Argentine economy were considered more important. Argentina was a major customer for British military exports, including jet aircraft and warships. But getting the British Parliament to sign off any agreement to hand over sovereignty to Argentina was a different matter. A sovereignty transfer agreement floundered in 1968 after it failed to gain Parliamentary support.

The first indication that the Argentine military government, or Junta that had come to power in a 1976 coup d'état might resort to armed force to seize the Falklands came to light in 1977. And when the British government learnt that an invasion seemed possible, a nuclear attack submarine, HMS *Dreadnought*, was dispatched to the South Atlantic. After the submarine arrived on station, news of her presence was leaked to the Argentine military by the British overseas intelligence agency, MI6. Argentine naval chiefs who had been pushing for military action backed down when their submarine commanders warned them that their conventionally powered boats were no match for *Dreadnought*.

In 1977 the then Prime Minister James Callaghan dispatched the nuclear powered submarine, HMS *Dreadnought*, to the South Atlantic to deter a threatened Argentine invasion, under the code name *Operation Journeyman*. *(No.10 Downing Street)*

The British Foreign Office deliberately played down the incident for fear of damaging relations with Argentina. There was no mood to humiliate the Junta when Britain's diplomats wanted to re-start negotiations and strike a deal with Buenos Aires.

When Margaret Thatcher's government came to power in 1979 there was another push to resolve the dispute with Argentina. The new Conservative foreign secretary, Lord Peter Carrington, was persuaded by his officials that the time was right to push for a lease-back deal.

But again, there was little support in Parliament for such a deal. The Junta was staging a brutal clampdown on its domestic opponents, known as the Dirty War. Tens of thousands of people were rounded up and imprisoned in brutal conditions. Up to 30,000 opponents of the Junta disappeared and are believed to have been killed by the military's death squads. Handing over 1,600 British citizens to be ruled by such a regime was opposed by British MPs from both sides of the house. Yet there was little concern in the British government that the impasse might lead to war.

However, the Falklands were only garrisoned by fewer than a hundred Royal Marines and the only naval presence was the ice patrol ship HMS *Endurance*. The truth was there was little to stop the Junta invading whenever they wished.

COMMANDING THE FALKLANDS WAR

The Loneliness of Command

To understand much of what happened in the Falklands War it is important to consider that it took place in a communications era that was more akin to World War Two than our modern world of satellite telephones, e-mails, and social media.

In some cases, it took days or weeks for crucial messages to be passed and received by senior commanders on ships spread out across the South Atlantic. Only a handful of rudimentary satellite radios were available to the British and the Argentines had none at all. There were no video conferencing links, streaming video, or email to send high resolution satellite reconnaissance photographs of enemy positions. Some warships were equipped with then-new data links to share radar and submarine tracks, but the technology was in its infancy and often proved unreliable. Long distance communications had to be sent by highly formatted signals that had to be physically typed into message machines.

This intelligence and communications gap was highlighted by the issue of satellite intelligence. It was widely assumed that the Americans would provide their British allies with huge quantities of images taken by their network of spy satellites. However, it transpired that hardly any of them orbited over South America or the Falklands. Also, the South Atlantic climate meant that

Woodward sailed from Gibraltar on HMS *Antrim* before transferring his flag to the carrier HMS *Hermes* for the rest of the campaign. *(DPL)*

Rear Admiral Sandy Woodward commanded the British naval task group in the South Atlantic throughout the Falklands campaign. *(MOD)*

for most of the war key locations, such as Port Stanley or Argentine airbases, were shrouded in cloud preventing the US spy satellites from taking any useful pictures. Even when the Americans could get decent pictures, the only way they could be delivered to the British task group was for hard copy prints to be flown to the airbase on Ascension Island and then parachuted to Royal Navy warships in the South Atlantic. There was no real-time surveillance of the Falklands. Not surprisingly, Royal Navy officers found the 1981 edition of the famous *Jane's Fighting*

Ships naval reference book to be their best source of intelligence on the Argentine navy.

This was still the era of paper maps and nautical charts, but these often proved to be hopelessly out-of-date or inaccurate. Actually sending someone to look at a beach or mountain to see if it could be crossed or was defended was critical to success or failure. These reconnaissance missions took time, effort and, in many cases, lives. This phenomenon seems so obsolete to modern observers but at the time was part of the normal business of war.

Commanders, like Britain's Rear Admiral Sandy Woodward or Argentina's Brigade General Mario Menéndez, made split second decisions based on flimsy information that was often rendered out-of-date when new intelligence arrived days or weeks later. This was the loneliness of command, exercised to the extreme.

The gathering, analysis, and dissemination of intelligence was crucial to how the commanders on both sides fought the war. Once established in the Falklands, the Argentines soon discovered they had very little information about where the British were or what they were doing, Their ageing maritime patrol aircraft just could not get close enough to the British task group to provide useful intelligence. This crippled their response to the British landings after May 21. Brigade General Menéndez's best source of intelligence was often sending an officer up onto the hills around Port Stanley to look for British warships through binoculars.

The British had a huge intelligence advantage. The eavesdropping agency GCHQ had cracked both the Argentine diplomatic cables traffic and the radio codes of the Argentine navy. Within hours of key messages being sent by the Junta in Buenos Aires they had been read by the British code breakers in Cheltenham.

The Cabinet in London often had advance warning of Argentine moves in the run-up to the war and once the Task Force approached the Falklands, the Ministry of Defence had early warning of enemy naval moves.

However, the precarious communications with the Task Force in the South Atlantic meant it often took hours or days for this war-winning intelligence to reach those who needed it. The events leading up the sinking of the ARA *General Belgrano* epitomised this phenomenon. In the aftermath of the war, critics of the decision to sink the Argentine ship made the case that when the British Prime Minister Margaret Thatcher and her senior military commanders ordered the ship to be sunk, they were in possession of details of both a Peruvian peace plan and orders for the Argentine navy to return to port. A whole industry of conspiracy theories developed. It turned out to be less clear cut. All the participants were working on out-of-date information, and no one had the full picture.

At crucial moments in the war, the commanders found themselves out of communications and ended up resorting to what is euphemistically dubbed 'best military judgement'. The Falklands war was definitely a conflict fought before the modern information era.

Major General Jeremy Moore went ashore on the Falklands at the end of May to direct the final British assault on Port Stanley. *(DPL)*

Brigadier Julian Thompson (far right) with the key staff officers of 3 Commando Brigade before they embarked on HMS *Fearless* to head to the South Atlantic. *(DPL)*

San Carlos Water under Argentine air attack in the days after the British landings on May 21. *(DPL)*

WAR ON SEA

Naval Action in the South Atlantic

Many sailors on warships in the South Atlantic faced experiences that were little different from their predecessors in World War Two. They had to man their stations in extreme weather, waiting for hours or days at a time for enemy aircraft and submarines to strike. It was cold, stamina-sapping and at times terrifying.

At the same time, inside Royal Navy warships' operations rooms, or ops rooms as they were known, a more 20th century war was underway as radar, sonar, and electronic warfare operators peered into screens looking for fleeting hostile contacts approaching the task group. There were dozens of false alarms every day, prompting crews to swing into action and go to defence stations. Investigations soon led to most threats being downgraded but not before sailors had been turned out of their bunks, guns manned, and lookouts posted. The uncertainty played on sailor's nerves. Often only the camaraderie and dark humour of their shipmates kept them going. A handful suffered nervous breakdowns.

Once the British nuclear submarine HMS *Conqueror* sank the cruiser ARA *General Belgrano*, the war turned into a duel between the Royal Navy and Argentine fighter pilots.

On the decks of Royal Navy warships crews manned 40mm Bofors guns, 20mm Oerlikon cannons and 7.62mm General Purpose

The aircraft carriers, HMS *Hermes* and HMS *Invincible*, were central to the British naval campaign. *(MOD)*

Machine Guns ready to start filling the sky with shells and tracer bullets. There was little prospect of downing a Mirage or Skyhawk jet flying at hundreds of miles an hour, but it was hoped the explosions and tracer fire would be enough to make the Argentine pilots pull up or misjudge their bomb runs.

Deep inside the warships the ops room staff were fighting a quite different type of war. The ships' radar operators were scanning the horizon trying to pick up the approaching Argentine jets and then target them with long range surface-to-air missiles. The Argentine pilots flew as close to sea as possible to hide their positions from the British, to reduce the reaction time of the Royal Navy missile operators. New data link technology, in theory, allowed all the British warships to automatically share radar track information so ops room staff could be rapidly warned of threats. However, the concept was still in its infancy, and it took highly trained operators to understand properly the nuances and quirks of how it worked.

Sitting next to the radar operators were electronic warfare specialists monitoring detectors that picked up and identified Argentine radar emissions. The infamous Etendard strike jet and its sea skimming Exocet anti-ship missile both transmitted distinctive radar signals that could be identified by equipment on the Royal Navy warships. So, when they were detected the ops rooms staff had to rapidly swing into action, alert their comrades on board as well as other ships of the task group. Crews would start firing off clouds of aluminium strips called chaff to try to decoy the Exocet missiles away from their targets. Gunners would try to engage

HMS *Valiant* was one of five British nuclear-powered attack submarines that dominated the South Atlantic from May 2 onwards. *(DPL)*

the missiles and crew members would close watertight doors before bracing for impact.

Argentine jets were approaching the British ships at speeds far in excess of World War Two propeller aircraft so within minutes of being detected they could appear overhead. The Exocet missile flew nearly at the speed of sound so British crews had even less time to react once they had been detected. To stand any chance of engaging these threats, missile crews had to rapidly spring into action. A fraction of a second could make the difference between life or death.

The Falklands war was the first large scale conventional naval engagement since World War Two. Only a handful of commanders and sailors on either side had actually seen action so they had little understanding of how the battle would unfold. The British had taken part in scores of NATO exercises, but they had never come under fire for real or seen what happens when a ship is actually hit by a missile or bomb. The Argentines had even less training.

Once the first Argentine and British ships were hit and sunk, the reality of naval war began to sink in. Commanders and sailors had to sharpen up or risk death. The Battle for the Falklands was no longer an exercise in diplomacy, it was a fight to the finish.

Type 42 air defence destroyers, such as HMS *Coventry*, fielded the Sea Dart air defence missile system but it proved unreliable when used in action off the Falklands. *(US Navy)*

The Sea Harrier jump jet dominated the skies over the Falklands. *(MOD, via David Oliver)*

WAR IN THE AIR

Aerial Combat over the Falklands

Aerial combat over the Falklands pitted Argentine and British pilots against each other in a deadly duel. They were flying 1960s and 1970s jets equipped with radars and guided missiles, but survival depended on split second reactions and keeping a constant eye on their fuel gauges.

The tactical scenarios faced by the British and the Argentinians were hugely different, but once in their cockpits their experiences were similar.

For the Argentine Mirage, Dagger, Skyhawk and Super Etendard pilots, combat missions started at one of their mainland air bases. Their mission was simple: to sink British ships. The bigger the ship, the better. This was easier said than done. Their intelligence on the location of the British warships was never very precise. Only once the amphibious landings were taking place did the Argentines have a firm idea of where to strike. They put every jet they could muster into the air.

Argentine navy personnel prepare to launch a Super Etendard on a Exocet strike against the British fleet in May 1982. *(DPL)*

The 500-kilometre flight towards the Falklands was always made at ultra-low level to avoid British radar surveillance and then they would try to hide behind the hills of West Falkland to give them the element of surprise on their final approach to the anchorage of the British amphibious shipping in San Carlos Water and Falkland Sound. They were at the extreme limit of their fuel endurance, so the Argentines only really had one chance to engage the British before they had to turn for home. What followed would be a terrifying rollercoaster.

After popping up over the final mountain range on West Falkland the Argentine pilots had a matter of seconds to scan the water below for British ships and then pick a target. This was just the moment when British anti-aircraft shells and missiles started to come towards them. Once committed to a target there was no room for manoeuvre. The Argentine pilot had to point his jet at the target, try to dodge incoming fire as best as possible and then drop bombs at the right moment. It took nerves and some skill to get bombs on target.

Even after pulling up from the attack runs, the terror was not over for the Argentine pilots. Positioned around the anchorage were Royal Navy Sea Harrier combat air patrols, which swooped down to try to engage the Argentine jets as they attempted to escape. With their fuel state at critical, there was no chance to turn and fight their pursuers. Their only option was to try to go low, merge with the hills and islands and hope they could outrun the Sea Harriers. The prospect of

Argentine navy pilots were the elite aviators of the country's armed forces. *(DPL)*

survival if they were shot down and landed in the freezing South Atlantic was slim. Weeks and months after the conflict the bodies of downed Argentine pilots were still being washed up on beaches around the Falklands.

Royal Navy and Royal Air Force Sea Harrier pilots had to make split second decisions on whether to engage their enemies. Fortunately, the Argentine jets rarely turned on their pursuers. There were often just too many enemy aircraft and split second decisions had to be made on which were the most important targets. Letting Argentine jets through could result in British ships being hit and sunk. Once committed to engaging a target, the British pilots had to dive to get

on their tail and then close to get missile lock. Keeping a fast moving jet in their sights, often at low level, for a vital few minutes was an extreme test of the British pilots' skills.

But just like their Argentine opponents, the Sea Harrier pilots were flying at the edge of their endurance envelope. They had to keep a constant eye on their fuel state and be ready to break off their combat air patrols to return to HMS *Hermes* or HMS *Invincible*. The extreme weather in the South Atlantic could change with little notice so returning to their carrier, when they were tired after a long patrol and with limited fuel, tested the pilot to the extreme. They could never relax until their Sea Harrier was safely back on deck.

Argentine naval aviator Owen Crippa flew his Aermacchi on a daredevil mission over the British fleet at San Carlos Water on May 21. *(Argentine Navy)*

British helicopter pilots flew into the heart of the battle outside Port Stanley to pick-up casualties. *(DPL)*

Royal Marines 'yomped' across the Falklands carrying all they needed to fight. (DPL)

WAR ON LAND

Fighting the Enemy and the Falklands Climate

For the soldiers who had to fight on the Falklands, the overriding impression was that they were not just fighting the enemy but the island's extreme climate. Almost every day it rained, the ground was sodden, at night temperatures hovered around zero and there were few buildings to provide shelter.

It was almost impossible for any of the soldiers living out on the mountains of the Falklands to stay dry. Colds and pneumonia were common. There were hundreds of cases of 'Trench foot', or immersion foot syndrome, from soldiers being unable to keep their feet dry. This harked back to the Western Front during World War One. It caused soldiers' feet to be covered in painful blisters that prevented them walking and in extreme cases led to inflections that could result in amputation of toes.

There were few roads to allow vehicles to deliver supplies to frontline positions, so soldiers had to live on field rations cooked on small stoves in trenches or bunkers. Both the British and Argentines struggled even to deliver field rations to their troops so often these ran short. Keeping fit and motivated tested even the most determined soldier.

Ground combat on the Falklands was fought by infantry. The rugged terrain meant that mechanised units just could not operate. Soldiers had to march to battle, with whatever they could carry on their backs. British Royal Marines called this 'yomping' and British Paratroopers preferred 'tabbing', a slang phase for a tactical advance to battle. In the extreme conditions, carrying more than 70lb of equipment was a challenge even for

Argentine conscripts spent weeks living in freezing and waterlogged trenches waiting for the British to attack. (DPL)

the fittest soldier. But for the British at least, marching helped them to keep warm.

The bulk of the Argentine army was positioned on a series of peaks overlooking Port Stanley and they just sat there in their trenches and bunkers for almost two months. They were cold, wet, and half-starved by the time the British launched their final ground attack in June.

Once the two armies closed for action the battle that unfolded was classic infantry combat. It culminated in June in a series of deliberate battalion-sized British night-time attacks on prepared Argentine positions. For the Royal Marines and British Paratroops this was the type of operation that was at the heart of their training. British infantry commanders and non-commissioned officers (NCOs) had the tactics and procedures for this type of attack drilled into them at a series of specialist battle schools on the Sennybridge training area in Wales or on Dartmoor in Devon. There could not have been a tactical situation more suited to the strengths of the British Army and Royal Marines.

These deliberate assaults were planned meticulously after detailed reconnaissance patrols had probed the Argentine defences and checked out the suitability of terrain around the enemy positions. The final ground assault was planned to take place under the cover of darkness to give the attacks the element of surprise. Once underway, specific enemy positions

were assigned to be captured by individual British companies, platoons, and sections.

If all went to plan, the assault force would get to within a few metres of their objectives and use grenades to kill and disable defenders. However, if discovered, the momentum of the assault had to be maintained by supporting troops and artillery laying down covering fire to force the defenders to keep their heads down to allow the attackers to advance to their objectives.

In the featureless Falklands there was little cover for infantry troops under artillery fire. Even Argentine troops in trenches soon began to take casualties from shell splinters from sustained British artillery fire. To rapidly bring down fire, Royal Artillery forward observation officers accompanied the forward wave of assault troops. Once they had pinpointed Argentine bunkers and trenches, they would call down a rain of shells that within minutes had silenced the defenders or forced them to flee. The Argentines tried to use their artillery to force British attackers to take cover, but they lacked night vision equipment to accurately spot their opponents ducking and diving between rocky outcrops.

Ground warfare in the Falklands was a brutal test of strength and motivation. The frontline infantryman on both sides was tested to the extreme and those who could keep advancing in the face of extreme conditions won the day.

Royal Marines digging in at San Carlos in the days after the British landing on May 21. *(DPL)*

British Paratroopers and Royal Marines lived off field rations cooked on improvised stoves in the days before their attack on Port Stanley. *(DPL)*

The 1981 defence review targeted older Leander class frigates and County-class destroyers for retirement. *(US Navy)*

THE NOTT REVIEW

Cuts to the Royal Navy

Conservative Prime Minister Margaret Thatcher has gone down in history as the 'Iron Lady', who was 'strong on defence' and 'always supported our boys in uniform'. It was not always so.

In the spring of 1981 Britain was mired in economic crisis. Unemployment had surged to over two million. The country's finances were in a precarious position and Mrs Thatcher ordered more cuts to public spending. The Ministry of Defence would not be spared the axe.

The newly appointed defence secretary, John Nott, set about finding ways to save money. Nott was a former officer in the Gurkhas and a barrister. He had a reputation for having a sharp mind but was completely unsentimental about Britain's military institutions.

Nott had received secret intelligence reports from the Americans that the Soviet naval threat was exaggerated, particularly the power of Moscow's surface fleet. Consequently, Nott set his target on the Royal Navy's surface fleet and, in particular, its aircraft carriers which seemed less important in any potential battle against the Soviet submarine threat. Scarce resources would be channelled into building five more nuclear-powered attack submarines and equipping them with Harpoon anti-ship missiles, as well as buying more Nimrod MR2 anti-submarine aircraft and guided Stingray torpedoes. The RAF and the British Army would be focused on building up NATO's presence in West Germany, receiving new Tornado and Harrier jets and new Challenger tanks, respectively.

To pay for all this new hardware, the Royal Navy surface fleet of 59 frigates and destroyers would be cut to around 50, with older Leander and Rothesay class frigates and County class destroyers being withdrawn from service rather than upgraded. Plans for new classes of anti-aircraft destroyers were put on hold and no more Type 42 destroyers were to be ordered. The aircraft carrier force would shrink from three to two, with the old HMS *Hermes* and new HMS *Invincible* being put up for sale, despite the latter ship only having been commissioned in 1980. The two landing dock ships, HMS *Fearless* and HMS *Intrepid*, were also to be sold off without replacement, putting at risk the ability of the Royal Marines to mount major amphibious operations. The historic Chatham dockyard was to close, along with a string of naval support bases and fuel stations. Between 8,000 and 10,000 sailors would be lost. The whole package of cuts was rounded off with the proposed retirement, in 1982, of the ice patrol ship HMS *Endurance*, which was Britain's most prominent military presence in the South Atlantic region.

Defence secretary John Nott ordered the Arctic patrol ship HMS *Endurance* to be scrapped, saying it was no longer a priority for resources at a time of growing tension between NATO and the Soviet Union. *(K. Krallis)*

The historic Chatham naval dockyard was considered surplus to requirement in the 1981 Defence Review as part of a cost saving drive to make the Royal Navy more efficient. *(Rob Mitchell)*

backed her defence secretary. The cuts were announced in June 1981 and Nott told the Royal Navy that the disposal of the ships would go ahead at a rapid pace.

In February 1982, the Australian government agreed to buy HMS *Invincible*, and HMS *Hermes* was scheduled to go as soon as the new HMS *Ark Royal* was ready to replace her. This would leave the Royal Navy with just two Invincible class carriers.

The cuts, which the Argentine Junta took as a sign of British weakness, haunted Nott for the rest of his career. In October 1982 he was interviewed by Robin Day when the BBC's head inquisitor asked: "Why should the public on this issue believe you, a transient, here today and, if I may say so, gone tomorrow politician rather than a senior officer of many years' experience?" Nott unceremoniously removed his microphone and strode out of the studio.

HMS	Invincible
Ordered	April 17, 1973
Builder	Vickers Shipbuilding Limited, Barrow-in-Furness, England
Laid down	July 1973
Launched	May 3, 1977
Commissioned	July 11, 1980
Pennant	R05
Displacement	22,000 tons fully loaded
Length	689ft (210m)
Beam	118.1ft (36.0m)
Draught	28.9ft (8.8m)
Propulsion	4 × Rolls-Royce Olympus TM3B gas turbines providing 97,000hp (72,000 kW)
Speed	28kts (52 km/h; 32mph) max
Complement	1,051 total, including 726 ship's company and 384 air group personnel
Armament	Sea Dart SAM
Aircraft carried	8 x Sea Harrier; 12 x Sea King HAS5

Not surprisingly, the leadership of the Royal Navy were outraged when the loss of so much of their fleet was proposed and the last ever navy minister, Keith Speed, resigned in protest.

The First Sea Lord, Admiral Sir Henry Leach, was seething and demanded a meeting with the Prime Minister. According to a declassified account of the meeting, the head of the navy told Thatcher: "he wished to emphasise the most serious miscalculation which we would be making [if] we disregarded the deterrent effect of a major maritime capability in peacetime."

The Foreign Secretary, Lord Peter Carrington, also raised concerns about the loss of HMS *Endurance*, telling the Prime Minister in another secret memo that the withdrawal of the ship "would be interpreted by both the [Falkland Islanders] and the Argentines as a reduction in our commitment to the islands in our willingness to defend them."

Nott was unmoved and told Mrs Thatcher that he was not going to risk a row with the Treasury over the cuts. The Prime Minister

Two Royal Navy aircraft carriers and their Sea Harrier jump jets were earmarked for the chop by Defence Secretary John Nott. *(US Navy)*

THE JUNTA AND 'LAS MALVINAS'

The Road to War

Argentina's road to war began in earnest on December 8, 1981 when the leader of the Junta was toppled in an internal coup d'état. General Roberto Viola was replaced by another Ejército Argentino (EA - Argentinian Army) man, General Leopoldo Galtieri.

However, the bombastic Galtieri was not the real driving force of the new Junta. That honour belonged to the head of the Argentinian Navy, Admiral Jorge Anaya. However, he could not take the reins of power himself, because the Armada de la República Argentina (ARA) was considered the junior service in the nation's military hierarchy. The new president rarely produced original ideas and relied on Anaya when making important decisions. The navy commander was a strident nationalist and virulent anti-communist. He had been a leading figure in the Dirty War against domestic opponents and was determined to establish Argentina as the leading South American power, eclipsing neighbours Chile and Brazil. Anaya was bolstered by the election of US President Ronald Reagan, and he was keen for Washington to recognise

Argentina as a key ally in Reagan's global struggle against the 'Evil Empire' of the Soviet Union.

Soon after Reagan came to power in January 1980, the US dropped many of the sanctions and arms embargoes which had been imposed by former Democratic President Jimmy Carter because of human rights abuses during the Dirty War. In return, Argentina offered to help the US fight its covert wars against pro-Soviet and pro-Cuban influences in central and south America. This boost to Argentina's status would be completed by the return of las Malvinas to the motherland - so thought Anaya and his fellow 'Malvinistas' in the Junta.

Within days of taking power, Anaya convinced Galtieri to authorise covert planning for a military operation to capture the Falklands. The decisions by the British government in June 1981 to run down the Royal Navy and withdraw HMS *Endurance* convinced the Junta that they would meet only token resistance. The Argentine foreign minister, Dr Nicanor Costa Mendez, was brought into the planning and instructed to launch an initiative that would

build diplomatic support in the United Nations and Organisation of American States for Buenos Aires. It was to be conducted in such a way that Britain could never agree to Argentina's terms and would paint London as being unreasonable. *Operation Rosario* was tentatively planned to take place at the height of the South Atlantic winter, between June and September 1982. By this point John Nott's naval cuts would have emasculated the Royal Navy and the winter weather would have made it impossible for the British to risk any sort of counter strike.

Ahead of the main operation to capture the Falkland Islands, Anaya had developed his own navy-led plan to stage a fait accompli to seize the British dependency of South Georgia,

An abandoned whaling station at Leith on South Georgia was the focus of the first phase of the Argentine navy's planning to remove British rule from the islands. *(Markabq)*

General Leopoldo Galtieri was nominally head of the Argentine military government or Junta, but he was often described as being easily manipulated by Admiral Anaya and other ultra-nationalist 'Malvinistas' officers. *(Presidencia de la Nación Argentina)*

700 nautical miles to the east of Port Stanley. This was to be repeat of the seizure in 1976 of uninhabited Southern Thule island, to the southeast of South Georgia. Argentine troops had landed on the frozen island and the British had just ignored them. Anaya calculated that the British would have little option but to accept Argentine control of South Georgia. An Argentine businessman, Constantino Davidoff won a

contract to remove scrap from a disused whaling station on South Georgia and Anaya made sure naval intelligence operatives went along with the scrap metal men. They were transported to South Georgia aboard a navy ice breaker and a corvette was provided to escort them.

Negotiations between British and Argentine diplomats opened in New York in February 1982. As planned, the Junta declared the British proposal for a joint commission to decide the fate of the Falklands to be unacceptable. At the beginning of March, the Foreign Office in London called a crisis meeting to respond. Foreign secretary Lord Carrington decided not to repeat the exercise of 1977 when a nuclear submarine was dispatched to the South Atlantic. The Ministry

of Defence then turned down a request to postpone the withdrawal of HMS *Endurance*. The first chance to reinforce the Falklands was lost. There would be no repeat of the pre-emptive deployment of HMS *Dreadnought*.

Just two weeks later *Operation Alpha* was executed when Davidoff's 60 scrap merchants landed on South Georgia and, in an act of provocation, raised the Argentine flag. Davidoff's team had also refused to have their passports stamped by the British Antarctic Survey representative on the island, claiming they did not need British permission to land on Argentine soil. In London, newspaper headlines started to appear saying Argentina had invaded British territory.

The Argentine navy supply ship, the ARA *Bahía Buen Suceso*, carried the first group of scrap metal merchants to land on South Georgia on March 19, 1982, sparking the crisis. *(Argentine Navy)*

From his Government House residence in Port Stanley, Governor Rex Hunt, repeatedly pressed the Foreign Office in London to take a hard line with the Argentine Junta. *(Alex Petrenko)*

SCRAP METAL MEN LAND ON
SOUTH GEORGIA

The Spark for War

Railway timetabling has famously been blamed for the outbreak of World War One. In 1914 the German high command believed that their superior railway system would allow them to launch a pre-emptive strike against France and then switch their armies rapidly by train to the east to fight the Russians and Austrians. However, the logistics of mobilising and then redeploying the armies by train meant the war against the French had to be won in a matter of weeks if they were to capture Paris and avoid the prospect of fighting on two fronts. This calculation drove the Germans to rush headlong into war to ensure they could have all their troop trains in the right place, at the right time. It was a classic example of what became known as the escalatory ladder and, once underway, there was no escape.

In the build-up to the Falklands War, the time it took ships to sail around the South Atlantic had a similar effect. Buenos Aires and London could work out how long it would take for ships and submarines to sail the 8,000 miles from Britain to the Falklands, from Port Stanley to South Georgia and from Argentina to the Falklands. Once intelligence emerged of ships and submarines leaving port, it prompted reactions and counter-moves.

The arrival of the Constantino Davidoff scrap metal operatives on South Georgia on March 19, 1982 was the first step on the

HMS *Spartan* was ordered to the South Atlantic in the days before the actual invasion, but she was not sent early enough to reach the Falklands before Argentine troops landed on April 2. *(MOD)*

Prime Minister Margaret Thatcher soon became determined to send a naval task force to the South Atlantic in response to the Argentine invasion. *(Rob Bogaerts / Anefo)*

escalatory ladder. Prompted by newspaper headlines of an Argentine invasion, four days later the British government ordered HMS *Endurance* to sail to South Georgia from Port Stanley with 22 Royal Marines on board to evict Davidoff's men. To pre-empt the arrival of the British reinforcement, Admiral Jorge Anaya in turn ordered his 70 or so marines on the ice breaker ARA *Bahia Paraiso* to go ashore at Leith and establish a military base to protect the scrap merchants.

HMS *Endurance* arrived off South Georgia slightly ahead of the ARA *Bahia Paraiso* but was ordered to stand off and link up with the British Atlantic Survey team at Grytviken before mounting a reconnaissance mission to observe the Argentine presence.

Captain Nick Barker on HMS *Endurance* reported back to London that the Argentines appeared to have set up a permanent military base at Leith, which was in a bay 15 miles around the coast

Foreign Secretary Lord Carrington resigned after the Argentine invasion. Defence secretary John Nott also offered to resign but Mrs Thatcher said he should stay in post to oversee the formation of the British Task Force. (Dutch National Archives)

proceed. There was no question of calling off the attack. It was now or never. On his flag ship, Admiral Büsser had been waiting for a recall message but nothing arrived. Fate intervened in the shape of a huge South Atlantic storm which forced Admiral Büsser to radio navy headquarters on March 31 to say he was having to postpone the invasion until the morning of April 2. The message was intercepted by the British signals intelligence organisation GCHQ, providing London with the first hard evidence that the Argentines were actually going to invade the islands.

Operation Alpha – Argentine Forces Deployed to South Georgia, March-April 1982

Tactical Group 60.1
Commander: Captain César Trombetta
ARA *Guerrico* (Drummond-class corvette)
ARA *Bahia Paraiso* (ice breaker/supply ship), with embarked Forces

- 1st Marine Infantry Battalion (BIM 1) (60 men)
- Buzos Tácticos (14 frogmen, Lieutenant Commander Alfredo Astiz)
- 1 x Puma SA330L and 1 x Alouette helicopter

Mrs Thatcher quickly reached out to her political ally in the White House, US President Roland Reagan, to pressure the Junta into holding off their invasion. (White House)

from Grytviken. The Royal Marines were ordered to dig in at Grytviken while the government tried to work out what to do.

In Argentina, the Junta was alert to any sign that the British might be about to reinforce the Falklands and pre-empt *Operation Rosario*. A British Atlantic Survey ship carrying the scheduled rotation of Royal Marines from Montevideo, in Uruguay, had just set sail for the Falklands. A British civilian survey ship was also spotted by the Argentines leaving the Chilian naval base at Punta Arenas, at the southern tip of South America on March 25. It seemed that the British might be reinforcing the Falklands. The next day, the Junta decided they had to move forward with *Rosario*. Admiral Anaya was told to sail his task force as soon as possible to seize the Falklands unless a message to countermand the orders was sent. This would ensure operational secrecy was maintained. The task group sailed from the main fleet base at Puerto Belgrano on March 28 under the command of Rear Admiral Carlos Büsser.

The British Embassy in Buenos Aires cabled London to warn that the Argentines were manipulating the crisis and would not back down. On March 29 Foreign secretary Lord Peter Carrington met with Margaret Thatcher. They decided that a nuclear-powered attack submarine should be sent to the South Atlantic as soon as possible. At full speed it would take just under two weeks to arrive.

New reports emerged later that day that a Royal Navy submarine had sailed from Gibraltar, where a NATO exercise was underway, for the Falklands. It was false. HMS *Superb* was only returning home to Faslane but senior officials in Ministry of Defence did not issue a denial, thinking it would help deter an Argentine attack if they believed the submarine was on its way south.

In Buenos Aires, the Junta received a report from the Argentine Embassy in London about the news of the sailing of the submarine. *Operation Rosario* would now

The Royal Navy began mobilising its ships to head to the South Atlantic in the hours before Argentine troops landed at Port Stanley. (DPL)

OPERATION ROSARIO

Invasion and Occupation of Falklands

On March 31, 1982 after the first GCHQ intelligence was received of the Argentine invasion, a crisis meeting was called by Prime Minister Thatcher. Late that evening a selection of ministers and officials gathered in her House of Commons office. The mood was grim and there seemed little that Britain could do to head off the move. By chance, the most senior military officer in London at the time was the head of the Royal Navy, Admiral Sir Henry Leach. He was called to the meeting, less than a year after he had clashed with the Defence Secretary John Nott over cuts to the maritime service.

Nott and others present said there was nothing Britain could do to retake the islands, but the Prime Minister turned to Leach and asked if the fleet could be sent to recapture the Falklands. He was made of sterner stuff than the defence secretary. "Yes, we could [retake the islands], and in my judgement we should," declared Leach. "If we don't or do it half-heartedly, and are not completely successful, we shall be living in a different country, which counts for very much less."

The Prime Minister instructed the Foreign Office to ask the Americans to try to call off the Argentines and she ordered Leach to begin preparing a task force to sail as soon as possible. Final orders would depend on what happened in the next 48 hours. US President Ronald Reagan was mobilised to telephone his Argentine counterpart on April 1, but General Galtieri refused to make any commitment to hold off his troops. The war would start in a few hours' time.

On board the amphibious landing ship ARA *Cabo San Antonio* during April 1, the commander of the Argentine Marine landing force, Rear Admiral Carlos Büsser, was issuing his final orders for the assault on the Falkland Islands.

While the aircraft carrier ARA *Veinticinco de Mayo* and a covering force of four destroyers set up a cordon around the Falklands, the amphibious landing force moved towards Port Stanley. The first troops would go ashore at first light on April 2, 1982.

On the Falkland Islands, Governor Rex Hunt received a telegram from the Foreign Office on the afternoon of April 1 warning him that

LVTP-7 amphibious armoured vehicles were soon driving through Port Stanley as Argentine Marines moved to surround the British garrison at Government House. *(Argentine Navy)*

Aircraft from the carrier, ARA *Veinticinco de Mayo* provided top cover for the Argentine invasion. Her A-4 Skyhawk jets were not needed. The Royal Navy was still 8,000 miles away. *(Ennio Chiecchio)*

A single Marine was sent to set up an observation post on Sapper Hill to watch for the arrival of the invasion force. A couple of sections were ordered to set up delaying positions on the road leading into Port Stanley town from the airport. The bulk of the British force was positioned around Government House on the western edge of the town.

Admiral Büsser's force outnumbered the British by almost 10 to one. The plan was to overwhelm the British with a demonstration of military power and force them to surrender as quickly as possible. The aim was for the operation to be as bloodless as possible, to limit diplomatic fallout and win over the islanders to their new rulers. It had been intended to conduct a joint operation involving an amphibious landing and a coup d'main air landing at the airport. However, when President Reagan telephoned General Galtieri, on the afternoon of April 1 to warn him not to invade, it was clear the element of surprise had been lost and the air landing operation was cancelled.

The opening move of the invasion was a raid by 84 navy special forces on the Royal Marines barracks at Moody Brook to the west of Port Stanley. They landed in rubber boats from the destroyer ARA *Santísima Trinidad* and advanced inland to their objective. They threw stun grenades to open the assault in a bid to surprise the sleeping occupants, but the Royal Marines had long gone.

The bulk of the Argentine landing force of the 2nd Marine Infantry Battalion was on the ARA *Cabo San Antonio* and it came ashore near Stanley airport in 20 LVTP-7 amphibious armoured vehicles and landing craft. A beach reconnaissance team had landed in small boats to make sure the coast was clear and plant beacons to guide in the assault vehicles. They then drove down the main road into Port Stanley to seize the governor's residence and other key points. As planned, the Royal Marines traded fire with the attackers, but they fell back towards Government House.

As the Argentine force surged into Port Stanley from the west, south, and east they soon had Government House surrounded. However, the Royal Marines were determined to make a fight of it. When the first group of Argentines approached, the British opened fire with every weapon they had. By the time the battle was over the Royal Marines had fired 6,450 rounds. Three Argentine soldiers were wounded, one fatally. The two sides now started trading fire

---

Buenos Aires Herald

EL HERALDO DE BUENOS AIRES

Phoenix Assurance Bicentenary

AGENTS SUD ATLANTICA

EJEMPLAR LEY 11.723

1782–1982

Founded 1876
106th Year — 2005 (new series)

BUENOS AIRES, SATURDAY, APRIL 3, 1982

16 Pages - Price: $ 5,000.-
Air mail $ 100.- surcharge

Thatcher pressured to fight

Argentina recovers Malvinas by force

A group of soldiers raise the Argentine flag at dawn yesterday on the Malvinas islands. (DYN photo supplied by the Argentine Navy)

ARGENTINA yesterday unilaterally put an end to a century and a half of vain negotiations to establish its right to govern the Malvinas islands by sending in a 4,000-man invasion force to take them over from their British administrators.

The pre-dawn landing included members of the three Argentine armed forces who easily overcame the handful of British troops stationed at Port Stanley, the Malvinas capital.

There was, however, armed resistance to the occupation, in which one Argentine officer died and another officer and an enlisted man were injured.

The Argentine Navy High Command reported yesterday afternoon that during the landing of the first wave of Argentine Marines, there was a firefight with the British Royal Marines. During the fighting, Captain Pedro Giachino, "who advanced heroically at the head of his men" on the British positions, was shot dead. Wounded were Navy Lieutenant Diego García Quiroga and Petty Officer Ernesto Urbina.

The operation was termed a complete success by the Argentine military who announced that the islands with their 1,900 inhabitants were under complete Argentine control following the surrender of British Governor Rex Hunt, who was earlier reported to have ordered the Royal Marines to cease resistance.

Argentine naval sources indicated last night that military protocol had been observed to the utmost, with the British personnel and island residents being treated with total consideration by the occupation force. The sources said that orders were also strict for the treatment of the British flag which was reportedly granted upon its removal the same respect given the Argentine colours which were run up.

On securing the islands the junta put out a communique in which it stated that "a long period of fruitless negotiations has come to an end" and added that the "Argentine people ...feel the happiness of having obtained just recourse on their demands for (recognition of) their legitimate rights."

The communique then went on to say that the junta, "as the supreme organ of state, informs the people of the Argentine nation that today the republic, through the armed forces, (which) carried out a successful joint operation, has regained the Malvinas, the South Georgia and Sandwich islands for the national patrimony".

The junta later in the day announced that it was ordering the evacuation of British military and administrative personnel which had been serving in the Malvinas. These people were expected to be flown to a British diplomatic mission elsewhere in Latin America. The Argentine Air Force would, the junta indicated, take care of the evacuation, shipping the British subjects out of Comodoro Rivadavia.

In London, British Prime Minister Margaret Thatcher called an emergency session of her cabinet as the British Royal Navy began feverish work to muster a naval task force to send to the south Atlantic, but last night at press time, she had apparently still not taken a definite decision as to whether or not to fight to regain control of the islands.

Sources in London made it clear that some British ships were already on their way to the islands while London worked at preparing a bigger more powerful strike force.

Meanwhile Mrs Thatcher faced a political storm which was brewing in parliament as the morning newspapers were last night preparing editions which would call on her to make the decision to go to war to wrest the islands from Argentine control.

The rightwing Daily Express published a frontpage photo of a group of islanders with the caption: "Our loyal subjects—we must defend them".

The Sun, a conservative tabloid, said simply, "It's war!" in an exclamation which covered most of the front page.

The Daily Mail opted for "Shamed" as its main headline, while The Times, the voice of the British establishment, urged that further efforts to resolve the conflict by diplomacy should be made "only as a prelude to taking action".

The Times added: "We still have one of the world's most powerful navies, including a number of nuclear-powered submarines, one at least of which is almost certainly now close to the scene."

President Galtieri and the military junta made it clear in their statements yesterday after the successful occupation of the Malvinas that Argentina would answer with force any attempt by the British at a counterattack to retake the islands. (UP, Reuters, NA, DYN, and own sources).

Britain demands immediate withdrawal from islands

United Nations

BRITAIN asked the UN Security Council yesterday to demand the immediate withdrawal of all Argentine forces from the Malvinas islands following what it called a massive invasion.

Submitting a resolution and appealing for its unanimous adoption, Sir Anthony Parsons, Britain's chief delegate, said: "I cannot find words strong enough to express my government's condemnation of this wanton act of armed force."

The Argentine delegate, Eduardo Roca, replied that his government has recovered for its national sovereignty the Malvinas which Britain had wained since 1833.

He said there were no civilian casualties in the Argentine military action that ended "a situation of tension and injustice."

Argentina was prepared to negotiate its differences with Britain, but sovereignty over the Malvinas, off South America, was not negotiable, he said.

The 15-nation Security Council deferred a scheduled debate on Nicaraguan charges against the United States to take up the Malvinas crisis.

After hearing the British and Argentine statements, members adjourned. They were expected to meet later yesterday to consider the British resolution.

The resolution would have the Security Council demand an immediate cessation of hostilities, demand the immediate withdrawal of all Argentine forces and call on the Argentine and British governments to seek a diplomatic solution and respect the purposes and principles of the UN charter.

Through a statement by its president, the Security Council on Thursday night called on both sides to observe the utmost restraint and refrain from the use or threat of force.

Sir Anthony accepted that appeal, but Roca did not respond.

When the Security Council met yesterday Sir Anthony said Argentina had ignored the appeal by the council president, Kamanda Wa Kamanda of Zaire, and two appeals by UN Secretary General Javier Perez de Cuellar.

Sir Anthony yesterday called the Argentine action a blatant violation of the UN charter and of international law.

"It is an attempt to impose by force a foreign and unwanted control over 1,900 peaceful agricultural people who have chosen in free and fair elections to maintain their links with Britain and the British way of life," he said. (Reuters)

Thousands gather at plaza

PRESIDENT Leopoldo Galtieri, spoke to a crowd of about 10,000 people gathered yesterday afternoon opposite Government House in the historic Plaza de Mayo square.

He received an enthusiastic ovation as he appeared on one of the balconies of the Casa Rosada and spoke for several minutes.

The President's improvised speech was interrupted several times as the crowd clapped and cheered as he announced the country's recovery of the disputed islands.

Galtieri said his government and the Argentine people would accept talks with the British government following Argentina's forcible takeover of the islands, but "dignity and national pride will be maintained at all costs."

(Continued on page 7)

There was national euphoria in Argentina in the wake of the seizure of the 'las Malvinas'. *(DPL)*

---

an invasion could be expected the following morning. It concluded by saying, "you will wish to make your dispositions accordingly." The governor later complained that no one in London wished him the "best of British" or expressed concern for the welfare of the Royal Marine garrison or the islanders. Hunt and his military commander, Major Mike Norman, now knew they were on their own.

The British garrison, dubbed Naval Party 8901, consisted of 76 Royal Marines and nine Royal Navy sailors left behind by HMS *Endurance*. They had no heavy weapons, artillery, or armoured vehicles. The local volunteers of the Falkland Islands' Defence Force were told to stay at home. Hunt and Norman knew the battle was doomed before it started and wanted to minimise casualties among the civilian population.

Hundreds of Argentine army troops were soon arriving by air to complete *Operation Rosario*, as the mission was code-named. *(Argentine Navy)*

Argentine naval special forces led *Operation Rosario* and are seen here collecting the weapons and equipment of the Royal Marines after the fall of Port Stanley. *(DPL)*

On South Georgia another small contingent of Royal Marines were preparing to resist a much larger Argentine force. *(Aah-Yeah)*

The Royal Marines shot down a Puma helicopter that rashly flew over their position on South Georgia. *(Brocken Inaglory)*

and Hunt took shelter under his desk, but it was obvious to the governor and his military commander that this was a futile exercise. Government House was made of wood and provided little protection. Norman told Hunt they had no weapons that could take on the Argentine LVTP-7 and artillery. They decided to surrender.

A truce was called and Admiral Büsser approached Government House under a white flag. The tall, dapper Argentine admiral was summoned into the governor's office. Hunt, who was five feet six inches tall and dwarfed by the Argentine admiral, was not overawed, telling Büsser: "This is British territory. We don't want you here. You're not invited, and I want you to go and take your men with you."

Büsser was not impressed, and he made it clear in no uncertain terms what would happen if the Royal Marines kept fighting. Hunt and Norman ordered their men to surrender. They were marched out of Government House with their hands above their heads, graphically symbolising the end of British rule.

The Argentine Marines had now secured all of Port Stanley and already the first Argentine Air Force transport aircraft had started landing at the town's airport to deliver the first army troops who would become the island's new garrison.

Further to the east, the Argentine force on South Georgia was ordered to move on the former whaling station at Grytviken to mop up the 22 Royal Marines holding out there. The corvette ARA *Guerrico* and the ice breaker

ARA *Bahia Paraiso* sailed into King Edwards Cove to start putting ashore their marines on the morning of April 3. Lieutenant Keith Mills had deployed his small force on the hillsides around the cove and they were primed to fight. Legend had it that when Mills was ordered by London to 'not resist beyond the point where lives might be lost to no avail' he reputedly commented: "Sod that, I'll make their eyes water." He later said this was a media exaggeration.

When the first Argentines started to land in a Puma helicopter, the British were ready and waiting for them. The helicopter was raked with machine gun fire, and it limped away, crashing across the cove. Two Argentines were killed and four wounded. The ARA *Guerrico* now entered the bay to provide fire support, but she sailed too close to the British position. The Royal Marines opened fire with machine guns and anti-tank rockets, one of which hit the corvette's forward turret. One sailor was killed and five wounded.

After turning out of the bay, the corvette's captain changed tactics. The ship moved further off shore and started to blast the British positions with its surviving 100mm cannon and the surviving Argentine Alouette helicopter began ferrying marines ashore to a landing zone out of range of the British weapons. Mills realised that the game was up. He had satisfied British honour. Waving a white coat as a flag of surrender he approached the Argentine troops.

The surrender of Lieutenant Mills and his Royal Marines was not the end of Britain's

military presence in the South Atlantic. HMS *Endurance* had been playing a game of hide and seek around South Georgia trying to evade the two Argentine warships. She launched her Wasp helicopter to aid the Royal Marines at Grytviken but when it approached the high ridge overlooking the settlement the crew saw the two Argentine ships at anchor. Resistance was clearly over. Captain Nick Barker and his crew spent two days hiding in bad weather around South Georgia before making the dash north to try to rejoin the main British task force heading south. For more than two weeks *Endurance* was alone in the South Atlantic providing vital signals intelligence of Argentine moves.

Operation Rosario – Argentine Seizure of Falklands, April 2, 1981
South Atlantic Military Theatre
Puerto Belgrano Naval Base, Buenos Aires Province
Commander: Vice Admiral Juan Lombardo

Task Group 20 – Covering Force Commander: Commander José Sarcona
ARA *Veinticinco de Mayo* (Colossus-class aircraft carrier with 8 x A-4Q Skyhawk, 5 x S-2E Trackers)
ARA *Comodoro Py* (Gearing-class destroyer)
ARA *Comodoro Seguí* (Allen M. Sumner-class destroyer)
ARA *Hipólito Bouchard* (Allen M. Sumner-class destroyer)
ARA *Piedrabuena* (Allen M. Sumner-class destroyer)
ARA *Punta Médanos* (fleet tanker)

Task Group 40 - Amphibious Force Commander: Rear Admiral Carlos Büsser
ARA *Santísima Trinidad* (Argentine-built Type 42 destroyer. Flagship with 1 x Lynx HAS.23 helicopter)
ARA *Cabo San Antonio* (Argentine-built De Soto County-class amphibious landing ship)
ARA *Hércules* (Type 42 destroyer with 1 x Lynx HAS.23 helicopter)
ARA *Granville* (Drummond-class corvette)
ARA *Drummond* (Drummond-class corvette)
ARA *Almirante Irízar* (Icebreaker with 3 x Sea King helicopters)
ARA *Santa Fe* (Balao/Guppy-class submarine)
ARA *Isla de los Estados* (supply ship)

Amphibious Task Group 40.1
Amphibious Commandos Group, embarked on destroyer ARA *Santísima Trinidad* with inflatable boats (50-84 men)
Buzos Tácticos, embarked on submarine ARA *Santa Fe* (15 frogmen)
2nd Marine Infantry Battalion (BIM 2). 500 troops embarked on LST ARA *Cabo San Antonio* and ARA *Almirante Irízar*
Amphibious Vehicle Battalion 20 LVTP-7 amphibious armoured vehicles and five LARC-V wheeled vehicles embarked on LST ARA *Cabo San Antonio*
A Battery, Marine Field Artillery, with six 105mm howitzers embarked on LST ARA *Cabo San Antonio*
C Company, 25th Infantry Regiment of Argentine Army, airlifted by C-130 aircraft

HMS *Endurance* escaped after the fall of South Georgia and spent two weeks dodging Argentine naval patrols while collecting vital signals intelligence of Argentine naval movements. *(DagosNavy)*

Royal Marines march from their base in Plymouth to board coaches to take them to ships loading in the Devon city's naval base. *(DPL)*

THE EMPIRE STRIKES BACK

The Royal Navy Sails to the South Atlantic

A fter he left the meeting with the Prime Minister on the evening of March 31, Admiral Sir Henry Leach began to alert his senior commanders to be ready for action. The First Sea Lord had promised Mrs Thatcher that the Royal Navy could take back the Falkland Islands, so he was going to mobilise every ship, submarine, helicopter, and aircraft that was available to go the South Atlantic to do just that. The *Operation Corporate* codename was first used in messages to Royal Navy warships during the evening of April 1.

Ships in port around Britain were warned to get ready to sail and a large task force that was in port in Gibraltar for the annual NATO exercise *Spring Train* was told to lead the task group. Their commander, Rear Admiral Sandy Woodward, was alerted to take charge of the ships heading south.

By the time the Argentines had landed in Port Stanley on the morning of April 2, the Chief of the Defence Staff, Admiral Sir Terry Lewin, was back in London after a visit to New Zealand. He attended the first War Cabinet

HMS *Glasgow* was taking part in NATO exercises off Gibraltar when she was ordered to sail for the South Atlantic. *(US Navy)*

meeting late that day and recommended that the mission of the task force should be 'to cause the withdrawal of Argentinian forces from the Falklands and restore the British administration'. The Prime Minister adopted Lewin's suggestion. Mrs Thatcher would publicly announce the dispatch of the fleet the following morning during an unprecedented emergency debate in the House of Commons.

Operation Corporate was to be run from the Royal Navy fleet command post at Northwood in west London. The underground bunker was co-located with the Royal Navy's submarine operations centre and had a global satellite communications network to link it to warships and submarines around the world.

The Commander-in-Chief Fleet, Admiral Sir John Fieldhouse, was nominated the commander of Operation Corporate and his Task Force 317 staff would co-ordinate the mission over the next three months. Fieldhouse was a submariner and as a result of his success running the Falklands campaign would rise to head the Royal Navy and then be Chief of the Defence Staff. However, the precarious communications link back to Northwood meant that the day-to-day tactical action of the forces in the South Atlantic were left largely to Woodward, who was soon to be embarked on the aircraft carrier HMS Hermes as the flag ship of Task Group 317.8.

Woodward controlled all surface ships and air operations in the South Atlantic, but Fieldhouse retained control of nuclear attack submarine operations, keeping them under the command of Flag Officer Submarines at Northwood, Vice-Admiral Peter Herbert. Eventually, five of the Royal Navy's 12 attack boats would be sent to the South Atlantic. First to go was HMS Spartan, which headed south from Gibraltar on April 1 and HMS Splendid left from Faslane naval base on the Clyde later that day. Two more submarines, HMS Conqueror and HMS Courageous, departed from Faslane on April 4. They would arrive in the South Atlantic by the middle of April.

The immediate challenge facing Admiral Fieldhouse was getting the fleet to sea. The Prime Minister had promised the House of Commons that HMS Invincible would leave port in two days time. This was one deadline the Royal Navy could not miss.

Not one but two aircraft carriers left Portsmouth on April 5. HMS Invincible and HMS Hermes sailed out of the port's famous entrance.

THE FALKLANDS (MALVINAS) 1982
—— Argentina
—— British

(US Military Academy)

5-6 April Falklands Task Force sails

North Atlantic Ocean

EUROPE
London
Portsmouth
Gibraltar
AFRICA

ASCENSION Task Force Base

South Atlantic Ocean

PERU
BRAZIL
BOLIVIA
PARAGUAY
URUGUAY
CHILE
ARGENTINA

Atlantic Conveyor Sunk 25 May

Falkland Islands

HMS SHEFFIELD Sunk 4 May
General Belgrano Sunk 2 May
Total Exclusion Zone

SOUTH GEORGIA
SOUTH SANDWICH ISLANDS

Distances from airbases to Falklands;
1. Ascension Island 6000 KM
2. Trelew 1070 KM
3. San Julian 780 KM
4. Rio Gallegos 800 KM
5. Rio Grande 700 KM

Argentina invades the Falklands on 2 April and South Georgia on 3 April 1982

SCALE OF MILES
0 500 1000 1500 2000

Royal Marines joined HMS Hermes, for the journey to Ascension Island and then cross decked to amphibious vessels for the rest of the operation. (DPL)

Sea Harriers and Sea King helicopters were arrayed on their decks and hundreds of sailors in the dress uniforms lined the flight decks. Thousands of well-wishers lined the quayside to say goodbye and the event was broadcast live on television. This was a level of popular support unlike anything the Royal Navy had seen before. The sailing of the carriers had a global impact with the US publication Newsweek putting a photograph of HMS Hermes on its front cover under the headline, The Empire Strikes Back.

Admiral Woodward set off from Gibraltar in the County class destroyer, HMS Antrim, with nine other ships of Exercise Spring Train group on April 2. These ships were the advance guard of the task force.

In Portsmouth, the rush to get the carriers to sea meant that there was not time to load all the required stores, equipment, and personnel. A shuttle of helicopters was activated to deliver more supplies as the big flat tops sailed out into the Atlantic. Behind the two carriers

During April 1982, diplomatic efforts led by the Americans attempted to find a negotiated solution to the crisis. *(White House)*

came a wave of frigates, amphibious ships, and Royal Fleet Auxiliary supply vessels.

To signal that Britain was serious about re-capturing the Falklands, the whole of 3 Commando Brigade was mobilised to head south with the task group. The headquarters, under Brigadier Julian Thompson, embarked on the assault ship HMS *Fearless* which sailed from Portsmouth on April 6. Three days later the bulk of the brigade sailed from Southampton on board the requisitioned cruise liner *Canberra*. Also embarked were 600 Paratroopers from the 2nd Battalion, The Parachute Regiment. The liner was one of more than 40 commercial vessels that would be mobilised over the next three months to support *Operation Corporate*. Known as 'Ships Taken Up from Trade', or STUFT, they sailed with their civilian crew but with Royal Navy officers in command.

Onboard HMS *Antrim*, Admiral Woodward and his small staff had little hard intelligence to go on about the terrain and climate of the Falkland Islands and its neighbouring sea zones. The best source of intelligence on the Argentine Navy was the 1981 edition of *Jane's Fighting Ships*. On HMS *Fearless*, Brigadier Thompson, and the commander of the amphibious landing ships, Commodore Mike Clapp, were equally in the dark about what they would

face. There was no intelligence about the Argentine garrison on the Falklands or its equipment. They were helped by the arrival on HMS *Fearless* of Major *Ewen* Southby-Tailyour who had previously served as the commander of Naval Party 8901. He had extensively charted the island's beaches during his tour of the Falklands.

As the ships headed south, the Ministry of Defence sought permission from the United States Department of Defense for unimpeded access to Wideawake Airfield on Ascension Island. Although nominally a British Overseas Territory, the island's airfield, and extensive logistic facilities, including vital fuel bunkers, were owned by the Americans. Fortunately, the US Secretary of Defense, Caspar Weinberger, was very pro-British. Unlike some senior figures in the US administration who wanted the US to remain neutral, Weinberger immediately ordered that every assistance should be given to the Royal Navy.

US Navy-owned super tankers started to arrive to re-fill the fuel bunkers on Ascension Island. Soon US Air Force C-5 Galaxy and C-141 airlifters were landing at Wideawake to deliver new and more advanced Sidewinder AIM-9L dogfighting missiles for the Fleet Air Arm's Sea Harriers. Stinger hand-held air-to-surface missiles and satellite communications systems were delivered for the Special Air Service.

Satellite imagery and signals intelligence started to be delivered to the British by the American military but the terrible weather over the South Atlantic meant there were few clear satellite pictures of Argentine bases. Weinberger was keen to send an SR-71 Blackbird spy plane to dive under the cloud to photograph the Falklands for the British. He ordered one of the supersonic jets to a US air base on Puerto Rico, but the USAF could not persuade any South American countries to host the KC-135Q tanker aircraft to refuel the spy planes on their mission, so the Blackbirds never flew over the South Atlantic.

Over the next three months, Ascension Island would become the key logistic hub for the task force. The main groups of warships anchored off the coast to undertake final re-supply and cross-decking of personnel and equipment. The Royal Air Force set up a base of its giant Vulcan B2 bombers, Victor K2 tankers and Nimrod MR1/2 maritime patrol aircraft. An around the clock stream of RAF transport aircraft started to arrive at Wideawake to deliver people and equipment for the task force. A helicopter shuttle carried these out to the ships anchored off shore or were taken south in Hercules transports to be airdropped to ships and submarines. When Argentine Boeing 707s started to patrol towards Ascension Island a detachment of Phantom fighters was deployed to provide air defence. Briefly for a period in April and May 1982 it was dubbed the 'busiest airport in the world'.

By the middle of April, Admiral Woodward and his first echelon of ships had arrived off Ascension Island. Admiral Fieldhouse flew down to Ascension to hold a planning conference with

Woodward, Clapp, Thompson, and their staffs. They thrashed out the timetable for a possible landing on the Falklands, the naval and air tactics needed to isolate the Argentine garrison from its mainland bases and the size of any land force. The *Operation Corporate* commander knocked heads together and headed home with an outline plan for the coming campaign. The overriding imperative was to get any land invasion over and done before the start of the South Atlantic winter in June. This would require the landing force to go ashore in the third week of May. More troops would be needed if the land battle with the Argentine garrison turned into a prolonged struggle, so the British Army's 5 Infantry Brigade was alerted to head south and plans were made to requisition Britain's largest cruise liner, the *Queen Elizabeth II*.

Operation Corporate Chain of Command April to June 1982
Task Force 317
Commander: Admiral Sir John Fieldhouse
Deputy Land Commander: Major General Jeremy Moore, then Lieutenant General Richard Trant
Air Commander: Air Marshal John Curtis (all based in Northwood)
Commander Task Group 324.3
Flag Officer Submarines: Vice-Admiral Sir Peter Herbert (Northwood)
Commander Task Group 317.8 (Carrier/Battle Group)
Flag Officer, First Flotilla: Rear Admiral Sandy Woodward (HMS *Hermes*)
Commander Task Group 317.0 (Amphibious Task Group) Commodore Amphibious Warfare: Commodore Mike Clapp (HMS *Fearless*)
Commander Task Group 317.1
Commander Land Forces Falkland Islands: Major General Jeremy Moore
Task Unit 317.1.1
3 Commando Brigade: Brigadier Julian Thompson
Task Unit 317.2
5 Infantry Brigade: Brigadier Tony Wilson
Commander Task Group 317.9
South Georgia Group: Captain Brian Young
British Forces Support Unit Ascension Island
Commander: Captain Robert McQueen RN

HMS *Hermes*	
Centaur class aircraft carrier	
Builder	Vickers-Armstrong
Laid down	June 21, 1944
Launched	February 16, 1953
Commissioned	November 25, 1959
Displacement	28,000 tons
Length	226.90m (744ft 5in)
Beam	43.90m (144ft 0in)
Speed	28kts (52km/h; 32mph)
Complement	2,100 all ranks
Aircraft carried	Up to 28 Sea Harriers and nine Sea Kings

The newly appointed Foreign Secretary Francis Pym led Britain's negotiating effort. *(White House)*

Brigadier Julian Thompson of 3 Commando Brigade led the planning effort to work out how and where a successful amphibious assault on the Falklands could be made. *(DPL)*

FORTRESS MALVINAS

Argentine Army Build-up

General Leopoldo Galtieri visited the Falklands in early April to view the island's defences and he ordered more reinforcements to be sent to beef them up. *(Argentine Army)*

R ear Admiral Carlos Büsser and his Marines had barely been in control of Port Stanley a few hours when their replacements started to arrive by air. By the evening of April 2, the assault units had either loaded back on to their landing ships or had been flown back to the mainland on air force, or Fuerza Aérea Argentina (FAA), transport planes.

The new garrison was comprised of just under 1,000 men from the Argentine army's 25th Infantry Regiment. On the first day of the occupation, they spread out around Port Stanley, securing government buildings, and setting up security posts around the airport. Over the next couple of days, small detachments were flown by helicopter to outlying settlements to raise the Argentine flag and make sure no Royal Marines had escaped from Port Stanley.

On April 3, Brigade General Mario Menéndez flew out to Port Stanley to become the military governor of the islands. His mission was to establish an interim military government until a civilian administration could be set up. A small command staff accompanied General Menéndez to help him take over running the local government, police, and other services.

Menéndez was bombarded with instructions from the Junta in Buenos Aires on how to treat the local population of 1,800 farmers and fishermen. His priority was to win them over to the Argentine cause.

The one thing Menéndez was not expecting to do was to defend the Falkland Islands from a British amphibious landing. The Junta did not believe that the British would be foolish

enough to launch a mission to recover the islands, so did not prepare any contingency plans to deploy significant air, land, or naval forces to the Falklands to defend them.

The media coverage of the sailings of HMS *Hermes* and HMS *Invincible* from Portsmouth on April 6 was a major shock to the Junta. This prompted a series of crisis meetings

PUERTO ARGENTINO 31-5-82.

A serious incident ocurred recently during wich a vehicle requisitioned by Argentine Forces was damaged by a civilian. The civilian population of Puerto Argentino (ex-Stanley) are reminded that the Military Government will protect and respect them in every possible way as established by the Geneva Convention.

However the Military Government also wants to make it perfectly clear that any transgressions to the issued orders or any act of disturbance will cause the application or severe measures accordingly and also contemplated by the Military Law.

SIGNED
THE MILITARY GOVERNMENT

The Argentine military government put considerable effort into trying to win over the Falkland Islanders. *(Liam Quinn)*

C-130 Hercules transport aircraft opened a daily airlift of supplies and personnel to Port Stanley airport that remained open until an hour before the surrender on June 14. From the start of May all flights had to be made at night to avoid British Sea Harrier fighter jets. *(Chris Lofting)*

The Argentine navy commandeered the *Monsunen*, a 326 ton freighter owned by the Falkland Islands Company, to move troops around the islands. She was later beached after coming under attack by HMS *Brilliant* on May 23. (*Argentine Navy*)

Argentine Forces on Falklands – April 2 to June 14, 1982
Commander: Brigade General Mario Menéndez
Land Forces Commander: Brigadier General Oscar Luis Jofre
Naval Forces Commander: Rear Admiral Otara
Air Forces Commander: Brigadier General Luis Castellano

Agrupación Puerto Argentino (Stanley Sector)
10th Mechanised Infantry Brigade

Agrupación Puerto Litoral (Island Sector)
3rd Mechanised Infantry Brigade
Goose Green: 12th Infantry Regiment
Port Howard, West Falkland: 5th Infantry Regiment
Fox Bay, West Falkland: 8th Infantry Regiment

Air Component – Order of Battle
Active Airfields from April 2 to June 14, 1982
AFB Puerto Argentino (Port Stanley Airport)
AFB Condor, Goose Green grass airfield
NAS Calderon, Pebble Island grass airfield

Aircraft and helicopters deployed to the Falkland Islands from April 2 to June 14, 1982

Argentine Air Force
12 x IA 58 Pucará ground attack aircraft
Argentine Naval Aviation
6 x - MB-339A light attack aircraft
4 x T-34C-1 Turbo Mentor light attack aircraft

Argentine Army Aviation
Operated from AFB Puerto Argentino and field locations
601st Army Aviation Battalion
2 x Boeing CH-47C Chinook heavy lift helicopter
3 x Agusta A109A utility helicopter
9 x Bell UH-1H Iroquois transport helicopter
5 x Aérospatiale Puma SA330L transport helicopter

Argentine Coast Guard
1 x SA-330L Puma
2 x Skyvan

involving its senior leadership to try to work out what to do. It was decided to launch a reinforcement operation of the islands to give Menéndez the ability to defend them.

To show that the Junta was not cowed by the dispatch of the British task force it ordered an additional army unit, the 8th Regiment, and the 5th Marine Battalion to be flown out to the Falklands.

The British secured a United Nations Security Council resolution on April 2, calling on the Argentines to withdraw their troops from the Falklands. This led to the opening of negotiations, brokered by the United States, to try to resolve the situation. As long as the negotiations were underway, the Junta was convinced it was a sign that the British were not serious about actually landing on the Falklands and any further build up of troops could be put off. This blasé attitude changed on April 9 when the liner SS *Canberra* sailed from Southampton loaded with thousands of Royal Marines and Paratroopers onboard. It looked like the British were serious.

The Junta now decided to dispatch a full infantry brigade, the 10th Brigade, to the Falklands, with three more infantry regiments, supporting artillery, anti-aircraft guns, and even a squadron of armoured cars. Plans were made to ship them out to the Falklands but a deployment of this size by sea was not something the Argentine military had done before, and it took several days to organise. It was complicated by the British declaration of their maritime exclusion zone around the islands on April 14. This coincided with the arrival of the first two British nuclear-powered attack submarines, HMS *Spartan* and HMS *Splendid,* in the South Atlantic with orders to sink any Argentine warships within 200 nautical miles of the Falklands.

While most of the 10th Brigade troops flew to Port Stanley, avoiding the British submarine threat, their vehicles, supplies, and heavy equipment had to go by ship. It was decided

that the ships carrying this vital materiel would sail individually to make it more difficult for the British to find them and also make them appear to be civilian vessels. One of the biggest cargo ships ran aground and never made it out of Argentine territorial waters. The other arrived long after the troops had arrived by air, so the soldiers were sent to man defensive positions without field kitchens, tents, and engineering equipment to build bunkers or shelters. Much of this equipment never made it up to the frontline positions, leaving the soldiers to survive in bleak Falklands weather without shelter or enough food.

This precarious logistic situation was made worse on April 22 after a visit to the Falklands by the head of the Junta, General Leopoldo Galtieri, when he ordered a second brigade, 3rd Brigade, to be sent to the Islands. This was despite the protests of Menéndez, who

complained it was madness to send more troops when he lacked the means to feed and supply the ones that were already on the islands. His protests were over-ruled and by the end of April there were just under 13,000 Argentine military personnel on the Falklands.

To try to locate the British naval task group as it sailed south from Ascension Island, the Argentine air force launched its Boeing 707 transport aircraft on surveillance missions. The British nicknamed the plane the 'burglar' and the flights only stopped after Sea Harriers started intercepting them. (*Chris Lofting*)

REJOICE, REJOICE

Retaking South Georgia

T he first British warships arrived off Ascension Island on April 10 to find the small island a teeming logistic base with supplies stacking up around the airfield as the non-stop shuttle of Royal Air Force transport aircraft moved into high gear.

Captain Brian Young and the crew of HMS *Antrim* did not have time to catch their breath. He was ordered to sail the following day to take command of an ad hoc task group to head towards South Georgia. Accompanying HMS *Antrim* were the frigate HMS *Plymouth* and the tanker RFA *Tidespring*. They would soon be joined by the frigate HMS *Brilliant* and another tanker, RFA *Brambleleaf,* which was heading around the Cape of Good Hope from Kenya. The supply ship RFA *Fort Austin* had already sailed south from Ascension with orders to link up with the ice patrol ship, HMS *Endurance*, which had managed to evade the Argentine navy in the days after the fall of South Georgia.

A land component was waiting on Ascension Island to be loaded on Captain Young's ships,

South Georgia's unforgiving weather nearly scuppered the British mission to remove the Argentine garrison, after two Wessex helicopters were lost in snow storms. *(DPL)*

HMS *Endurance* joined forces with the Royal Navy task group led by HMS *Antrim* as it arrived off South Georgia. *(DPL)*

HMS *Antrim* led *Operation Paraquet* to South Georgia. The British participants in the mission soon renamed it *Operation Paraquat* after the famous weedkiller. *(MOD)*

including M Company of the Royal Marines, a Special Boat Service detachment, and D Squadron of 22 Special Air Service. Two troop-carrying Wessex HU5 helicopters were embarked on RFA *Tidespring* to land the assault force.

The British War Cabinet wanted the so-called Antrim Group to be in position as early as possible in case negotiations organised by the US Secretary of State, General Al Haig, failed.

Lying some 700 nautical miles to the east of Port Stanley, South Georgia was seen as an easy target because it was out of the range of Argentine land-based strike aircraft. However, Captain Young's ships were still highly vulnerable to Argentine corvettes armed with Exocet anti-ships and Argentine submarines, so they headed south under conditions of great secrecy.

Communication with the Antrim Group was precarious, and Captain Young was ordered to minimise electronic emissions. The written orders were air-dropped to the ships from an RAF Nimrod MR2 on April 13, with Captain Young being instructed to have his forces ready to land on South Georgia on April 21.

To make sure the coast was clear, the nuclear attack submarine HMS *Conqueror* was sent

The formidable Fortuna Glacier inflicted a major setback to the Special Air Service. Daring to win could not overcome mother nature's power. *(Michael Clarke)*

Royal Marines remained to garrison South Georgia after its liberation. *(DPL)*

ahead to patrol around South Georgia. And on April 20, an RAF Victor K2 tanker modified for maritime radar reconnaissance flew the first of three surveillance missions from Ascension to monitor the sea around the island. Four other Victors refuelled the surveillance aircraft as it headed south, and four more tankers made sure the aircraft could safely return to base. The aircraft spotted no Argentine warships in the path of Captain Young's task group. No other Argentine ships were spotted on two more Victor missions over the next week.

However, GCHQ picked up signals intelligence that the Argentine submarine

ARA *Santa Fe* was heading to South Georgia. The Argentine navy chief, Admiral Jorge Anaya, had ordered the submarine to head to the island on a re-supply mission for the garrison, despite orders from the Junta that the navy should concentrate on the defence of the Falklands and the mainland.

With diplomatic negotiations now deadlocked, on April 20, the War Cabinet ordered Captain Young to proceed with what was now co-named *Operation Paraquet*. The intelligence on the approach of the ARA *Santa Fe* meant he had to disperse his ships while plans were hatched to land troops on South Georgia.

The SAS commander proposed landing his force by helicopter on the Fortuna Glacier above the Grytviken settlement, where the main Argentine force was based, as a precursor for a surprise land attack. Captain Barker and Royal Marine officers warned that the extreme weather and terrain would doom landing on the glacier. The Royal Marines later accused the SAS of using their satellite radio to persuade the task force headquarters at Northwood to overrule them.

The Wessex HU5 flew 15 SAS men onto the glacier but disaster struck. A blizzard engulfed the SAS men, and they were forced to call for evacuation, as they desperately dug snow holes to shelter from the storm. Three helicopters headed out to rescue the stranded men. One Wessex HU5 was engulfed in a white out immediately after landing and crashed. Its crew and the SAS men were picked up by the other helicopters but the other Wessex HU5 also crashed soon after take-off. The remaining Wessex, HMS *Antrim*'s HAS3, made a desperate bid to recover the downed aviators and SAS men. All the survivors were found and eventually bundled aboard but they had to abandon all their equipment. On the night of April 22/23 another attempt to land an SAS reconnaissance team in two Gemini boats also ended in failure when the craft were swept out to sea in a gale. They had to be rescued by HMS *Endurance*'s Wasp helicopter.

Britain's operation to recover South Georgia seemed like it was heading for disaster and unless Captain Young could re-group all his ships and bring the 120 Royal Marines on RFA *Tidespring* into action there seemed little prospect of success.

During the evening of April 24, signals intelligence arrived reporting that the ARA *Santa Fe* was going to make a run into

British guided missiles blasted holes in the conning tower of the ARA *Santa Fe. (DPL)*

Lieutenant Commander Alfredo Astiz signs the surrender document in the ward room of HMS *Antrim*. Along with 189 military personnel and civilians captured on South Georgia he was later returned to Argentina, despite calls to face trial in France and Sweden for crimes against their nationals during the Dirty War. *(DPL)*

A relieved Thatcher strode out of 10 Downing Street to declare that Britain should "Rejoice, rejoice." It was one of the most memorable and controversial lines from the war, second only to the "Gotcha" headline that appeared in *The Sun* newspaper after the Argentine cruiser ARA *General Belgrano* was sunk.

Task Group 317.9	
Commander: Captain B.G. Young	
County-class destroyer	HMS *Antrim*
Rothesay-class frigate	HMS *Plymouth*
Type 22 frigate	HMS *Brilliant*
Ice patrol ship	HMS *Endurance*
Tankers	RFA *Tidespring* RFA *Brambleleaf*
M Company, 42 Commando, Royal Marines	
2 & 6 Special Boat Squadron	
D Squadron, 22 Special Air Service	
Mountain and Boat Troops SAS	

ARA *Santa Fe* (ex USS *Catfish*)	
Balao-class diesel-electric submarine	
Builder	Electric Boat Company, Groton, Connecticut
Laid down	January 6, 1944
Transferred to Argentina	July 1, 1971
Displacement	2,424 tons
Length	95.02m (311ft 9in)
Beam	8.31m (27ft 3in)
Speed	38km/h (20.25kts) surfaced, 16km/h (8.75kts) submerged
Complement	10 officers, 70–71 enlisted
Armament	10 × 21in (533mm) torpedo tubes, 24 torpedoes 1 × 5in (127mm) deck gun Bofors 40mm and Oerlikon 20mm cannon

Grytviken to unload its cargo. Captain Young now decided to strike. His ships would launch a massed helicopter attack on the submarine at first light the following day in the hope of catching her on the surface.

At dawn, the helicopters appeared over Cumberland Bay just as the submarine was making a run to the open water on the surface. First to attack was HMS *Antrim*'s veteran Wessex HAS3 which dropped two depth charges astride the submarine, peppering her with shrapnel and rendering her unable to dive. Two of HMS *Brilliant*'s Lynx helicopters now attacked with anti-submarine torpedoes, but they passed harmlessly under the submarine, which was now heading back to shore.

Two Wasps from HMS *Plymouth* and one from HMS *Endurance* made the final attack using AS-12 wire-guided anti-tank missiles. One of the missiles scored a direct hit on the submarine's sail and its crew were lucky to be able to beach her outside Grytviken.

Captain Young now mustered his land commanders, and they were ordered to mount a follow up attack to go ashore to capitalise on the grounding of the submarine. There were some 79 troops on the three British warships, including the survivors of the Fortuna garrison, a small SBS contingent and the Royal Marines command team. They all grabbed their weapons and prepared for a helicopter assault.

HMS *Antrim*, HMS *Plymouth* and HMS *Brilliant* now lined up outside Cumberland Bay ready to provide naval gunfire support for the assault force. A barrage was laid down on the hills outside the settlement to give the Argentines a taste of what was soon to be heading their way and it had the desired effect. The raised the white flag even before the British troops got within rifle range. With their submarine beached and no help at hand, they could see how hopeless their position was.

After the action, the Royal Marines and SAS disputed each others' roles in the action. One Royal Marine officer even accused the SAS troops of firing anti-tank missiles at an empty hillside and machine gunning elephant seals.

After the battle, when a senior officer asked the Royal Marine commander, Major Guy Sheridan, to recommend participants in the battle for gallantry medals, he declined to do so, saying "we had not come under [enemy] fire at any point."

Captain Young was now able to signal the task group headquarters in Northwood. "Be pleased to inform Her Majesty that the White Ensign flies alongside the Union Jack in South Georgia. God save the Queen."

South Georgia was the first territory to be re-captured from Argentine occupation. In London, Prime Minister Margaret Thatcher and her defence chiefs had been waiting nervously for five days for good news from Captain Young. The disaster on the glacier had made them fear the operation was going to be unsuccessful and would undermine domestic support for the campaign even before the main attack on the Falkland Islands had begun.

A Royal Navy firing party firing a salute over the grave of Petty Officer Felix Atuso of the Argentine Navy, shot on April 27 on board the ARA *Santa Fe* after he was mistakenly suspected of trying to sabotage the submarine. He was the only fatality during *Operation Paraquet*. *(DPL)*

INTO THE TOTAL
EXCLUSION ZONE

The Royal Navy tightens its Grip on the Falklands

By mid-April, the Junta was waking up to the approaching British task group and it had begun to mobilise its air and naval forces. Argentine air force and navy fighter and bomber aircraft were moved to airfields in the south of Argentina to bring them within range of the disputed region. Similarly, the navy formed its warships into task groups and began a round of intense training to prepare for action.

The Argentine plan was not to commit their main air and naval forces until the British were in the process of landing their troops on the Falklands. However, their ability to monitor the progress of the British fleet was severely hampered by a lack of modern maritime patrol aircraft, fully operational submarines, and long range radar on the Falkland Islands. They flew several sorties with Boeing 707 airliners over the South Atlantic in a bid to find the British fleet and navy P-2 Neptune patrol aircraft began scouring the waters around the Falklands as the naval force approached.

Rear Admiral Sandy Woodward set sail south from Ascension Island on April 18 on board HMS *Hermes* and other warships and supply vessels accompanied Woodward's flag ship on the voyage.

Sea Harrier fighter jets from HMS *Invincible* were to play a key role in the air defence of the British naval task group. *(Navy Wings)*

The initial objective of the task group was to impose a naval and air blockade around the Falklands to prevent any Argentine supply ships or aircraft sustaining the garrison. This was an essential precursor to any

British landing to recapture the islands, even through at this stage the War Cabinet had not explicitly authorised a full scale assault.

Woodward, and his immediate superior Admiral Sir John Fieldhouse, were both pushing for a commitment from the War Cabinet to go ahead with the landing. The South Atlantic winter was approaching, which would make it impossible for the Royal Navy to sustain its warships off the coast of the Falklands or put troops ashore. As far as the military commanders were concerned, the clock was ticking and there was no time to lose. Negotiations were still underway under the auspices of the Americans, so Margaret Thatcher was not yet willing to formally order the first direct action against the Falkland Islands themselves.

Admiral Fieldhouse was determined to be ready to strike if diplomacy should fail. He had been to meet Woodward on Ascension Island, and they had agreed the plan. The British commanders had correctly worked out the Argentine strategy and were determined to try to lure out their air and naval forces so they could be whittled down ahead of the main amphibious landings.

Three nuclear attack submarines were positioned between the Falklands and the Argentine mainland to intercept any naval forays. Woodward's fleet was moving to patrol to the east of the Falklands and then launch its Sea Harriers to bomb targets around Port Stanley airport to close its runway. This operation would be preceded by a strike

HMS *Splendid* arrived off the Falklands in mid April, allowing the British to activate their maritime exclusion zone around the islands. *(MOD)*

HMS *Broadsword* steams past HMS *Hermes* as she prepares to launch Sea Harrier fighter jets on a combat air patrol. *(DPL)*

British Naval Forces in the Total Exclusion Zone – May 1, 1982
Task Group 324.3 Commander: Vice-Admiral Peter Herbert
Nuclear-powered Attack Submarines HMS *Spartan* HMS *Splendid* HMS *Conqueror*
Task Group 317.8 (Carrier Battle Group in South Atlantic) Commander: Rear Admiral Sandy Woodward
Aircraft Carriers HMS *Hermes* HMS *Invincible*
Type 42 destroyers HMS *Sheffield* HMS *Coventry* HMS *Glasgow*
County-class destroyer HMS *Glamorgan*
Type 22 frigate HMS *Broadsword*
Type 21 frigates HMS *Arrow* HMS *Alacrity*
Rothesay-class frigates HMS *Yarmouth*
Royal Fleet Auxiliary RFA *Olmeda* RFA *Resource* RFA *Appleleaf*

on the airport's runway by a Royal Air Force Vulcan bomber flying from Ascension Island.

After the first softening-up air strikes, Royal Navy warships were to close on the shore to begin bombarding coastal targets in a bid to make the Argentines think an invasion was underway. This would force them to commit their air force and give the British the opportunity to shoot their planes down with surface-to-air missiles and Sea Harriers. Amid this air and naval battle, British helicopters were to make night-time incursions on to the islands to land Special Air Service and Special Boat Squadron reconnaissance teams to locate the main Argentine troop concentrations and possible identify landing beaches.

When negotiations floundered in the last days of April, the war cabinet ordered Fieldhouse and Woodward to execute their plans on May 1. As a precursor, on April 30 the activation of a total exclusion zone some 200 nautical miles around the Falklands was announced by the British. A week earlier, the British had told the Argentines, via the Swiss Embassy in Buenos Aires, that any ships or aircraft, anywhere, considered a threat to British forces would be liable to attack.

The ocean going tug the ARA *Alférez Sobral* was operating in the exclusion zone in the first days of May as an intelligence gathering ship. She was attacked with Sea Skua missiles launched from Royal Navy Lynx helicopters on May 3. *(Matias Cosso)*

The mighty Vulcan was due to be retired by the RAF when she was called to fly the *Black Buck* bombing missions. *(USAF)*

OPERATION BLACK BUCK

The RAF Attacks Port Stanley

Flt Lt Martin Withers and his crew on their return from the *Black Buck 1* mission at Wideawake Airfield. *(Private Collection)*

The opening blow of the British campaign to retake the Falkland Islands was struck by a single Vulcan bomber of the Royal Air Force. At the time, *Operation Black Buck* was the longest range bombing mission ever undertaken at some 6,600 nautical miles.

To get one Vulcan down to Port Stanley required a massive air-to-air refuelling effort involving 11 Victors on the outward leg of the raid and three more to refuel the bomber as it returned to Ascension Island.

Operation Black Buck was controversial from the moment the RAF proposed the attack. The Royal Navy was not convinced it would work and if one of the Vulcans or Victors was lost it would hand the Argentines a propaganda victory. In the end the War Cabinet signed

off the on the plan. Putting the Port Stanley Airport runway out of action was a top priority as it would prevent the Argentine air force from operating fast jets from the location. The ability to do so would have made attacking the British carriers far easier than would be the case with mainland launched missions. It was felt the long distance raid might also force the Argentines to divert fighter aircraft to defend their mainland from future Vulcan strikes.

The raid launched late on the evening of April 30 with two waves of Victors taking off from Ascension's Wideawake Airfield, ahead of the two bombers assigned to fly the mission. One Vulcan was a spare in case the primary aircraft suffered technical problems. Just after take off, the cockpit window seal on the primary aircraft failed making it impossible for the crew to see out. They had to turn back and handed the mission over to Flight Lieutenant Martin Withers and his crew. One of the Victors also suffered a malfunction and had to be replaced by a reserve. The formation of remaining aircraft now headed south.

The Vulcan was refuelled six times and several of the Victors were also refuelled so they could continue south to accompany Withers'

The two *Black Buck* Vulcans at Wideawake Airfield. *(via David Oliver)*

The *Black Buck* Vulcans relied on air-to-air refuelling from Victor tankers. *(MOD via Andy Thomas)*

for the safety of the British fleet, where Sea Harriers were on the deck of the carriers ready to scramble. When Withers was safely out of range, he broke radio silence and broadcast the codeword 'Superfuze' to signal a successful attack.

Withers' problem now was getting his Vulcan safely back to Ascension. The last two Victors were also dangerously short on fuel so additional tankers were scrambled to enable the aircraft to make it back to their base. A Nimrod MR2 was also launched to help co-ordinate the refuelling and all the aircraft eventually returned safely. Withers' aircraft touched down just before 3pm after 14 hours and five minutes in the air.

Avro Vulcan B2	
Wingspan	33.83m (111ft)
Length	32.16m (105ft 6in)
Height	8.26m (27ft 1in)
Max. takeoff weight	84,000kg (185,000lb)
Cruising speed	Mach 0.86
Armament	21 × 1,000lb (450kg) conventional bombs

aircraft until it was within striking distance of Port Stanley. The flight south had taken more fuel than expected and the final Victor in the refuelling chain would not have enough fuel to get back to Ascension Island, but the pilots decided to press on to the target.

As Withers approached the islands from the north, he dropped the Vulcan down to 300 feet to avoid Argentine air defence radars at Port Stanley. As he approached his target, Withers pulled the aircraft up to 1,000 feet to allow his bomb aimer to make a radar scan of the island to get a fix on the locations of the airport. With his heading confirmed, the aircraft's automated bomb-aiming system was activated, and Withers lined up for a pass over the airport at 10,000 feet. To defeat the Argentine radar-guided anti-aircraft guns around the airport, the Vulcan's crew activated their jammers. At 4.40am the Vulcan crossed the runway at 35° and the automated system released 21 of its 1,000lb bombs.

On the ground, the first the Argentines knew of the presence of the Vulcan was when the bombs started to explode. Windows were smashed in the airport control tower and other buildings. Three Argentine personnel were killed in the attack.

Once the smoke cleared the Argentines discovered a long line of craters across the

isthmus containing the airport, including one very large crater in the main runway. Withers had achieved his mission.

To the north, the Vulcan pulled a violent turn away from Port Stanley and headed

Aerial reconnaissance pictures taken by Royal Navy Sea Harriers on May 1 proved that *Black Buck 1* had landed one of its bombs on target *(DPL)*

Port Stanley airport after the *Black Buck* raid. *(Think Defence)*

 **AIR RAID**

HARRIER STRIKE

Aerial Battles Around Port Stanley

"I'm not allowed to say how many planes joined the raid, but I counted them all out, and I counted them all back." That was how the veteran BBC correspondent, Brian Hanrahan, described the first British Sea Harrier raid on Port Stanley on the morning of May 1, 1982.

Ministry of Defence censors refused to allow Hanrahan say how many jets had launched from HMS *Hermes* to take part in the raid, which occurred a few hours after the *Black Buck* Vulcan had delivered its bombs on to Port Stanley airport.

At first light, the task group commander, Rear Admiral Sandy Woodward, positioned his aircraft carriers in striking range of Port Stanley. His plan was to draw out the Argentine air force and navy so they could be engaged and destroyed. Eighteen Sea Harriers took to the skies, including four whose job was to fly a protective combat air patrol to keep any Argentine fighters at bay.

The first two Harriers over Port Stanley were equipped with photo-reconnaissance pods to take pictures of the damage caused by the Vulcan. Once lab technicians on HMS *Hermes* had developed the pictures Admiral Woodward was able to see for himself the impact of the RAF strike. Minutes after the recce jets made their pass, nine more Harriers roared across the airfield dropping three 1,000lb bombs each. A fuel store was set on fire and Argentine soldiers were forced to dive for cover. Anti-aircraft guns opened fire at the British jets, one of which took a round in its tail, but it was able

Sea Harriers launch from HMS *Hermes* to bomb the Falklands. *(MOD, via David Oliver)*

Sidewinder missiles and 1,000lb bombs being prepared for loading on the deck of HMS *Hermes*. *(DPL)*

to return safely to its carrier. The final three Sea Harriers raided the grass airstrip at Goose Green, dropping cluster bombs over a pair of Pucara ground attack aircraft as they were preparing to take off, putting both aircraft out of action. One Argentine pilot and six air force mechanics were killed in the carnage.

The next phase of Woodward's plan involved Royal Navy warships closing with the Falklands, while Sea Harriers flew combat air patrols ready to engage Argentine jets. The frigates HMS *Broadsword* and HMS *Yarmouth* were sent northwest of Port Stanley to hunt for the Argentine submarine ARA *San Luis* after British signals intelligence intercepted a radio message about the vessel. And HMS *Glamorgan*, HMS *Arrow* and HMS *Alacrity* closed to within seven miles of the coast and began to shell Port Stanley airfield.

The Argentine high command fell for the British deception and during the morning of May 1 orders were given to launch a major air and naval attack. A dozen Argentine air force jets – four A-4B Skyhawks, four Mirage IIIs and four Daggers - were launched. They tried to find the ships hunting for the ARA *San Luis* but failed to locate any targets. Two of the Mirage IIIEs fired missiles at what they thought were Sea Harriers, without success, before heading home. Two Argentine navy Turbo-Mentor propeller strike aircraft on a patrol looking for British helicopters

were spotted by Sea Harriers and had to violently manoeuvre to escape the British jets.

This was the warm up act for a major Argentine air force strike in the afternoon. More than 50 jets, including 37 armed with bombs designed to target ships, were launched simultaneously in a bid to swamp the British defences. The first three Daggers found the shore bombardment group of ships, dropping bombs around them and then making strafing runs with cannons. None of the bombs hit but a handful of crewmen were injured by shrapnel and cannon fire.

Minutes behind the Daggers were 24 Skyhawks but they did not find any British ships and a group of jets mistakenly bombed an Argentine supply ship off East Falkland. Fortunately for the crew, the bombs all missed or failed to detonate. Next up were six British-made Canberra B-62s, which flew straight into a Sea Harrier patrol and one of the Argentine Canberras was shot down by a Sidewinder air-to-air missile.

The Argentine bombers were escorted by pairs of Mirage IIIE, and Dagger jets armed with air-to-air missiles. These flew at medium level so they could use their radars to look for Sea Harriers. Throughout the afternoon the rival fighters played a game of cat and mouse. A dogfight ensued to the north of Port Stanley, in which two Sea Harriers jumped a pair of Mirages. Their Sidewinders found their mark, destroying one Argentine jet outright and damaging another. It limped towards Port Stanley in the hope of making an emergency landing, only to be mistaken for a British jet and was shot down by the air defences. Sea Harriers intercepted a pair of Daggers south of East Falkland and one was hit by a Sidewinder as it tried to escape.

On HMS *Hermes*, Admiral Woodward was pleased that his pilots had shot down three Argentine aircraft, damaged two on the ground and contributed to the loss of another. There was no time to be complacent though. British signals intelligence was passing the Admiral messages suggesting that the Argentine fleet was poised to attack.

HMS *Invincible's* Sea Harriers joined the attacks on Port Stanley and then stood ready to defend the task group. *(MOD, via David Oliver)*

British Aerospace Sea Harrier FRS1	
Crew	1
Length	14.5m (47ft 7in)
Wingspan	7.69m (25ft 3in)
Max Weight	11,339kg (25,000lbs)
Max Speed	1,188km/h (642kts)
Range	Strike role 463km (250nm); Fighter role 740km (400nm)
Armament	Two 30mm Aden cannon, four Sidewinder air-to-air missiles, various combinations of bombs or two Sea Eagle air to surface missiles.

Argentine air force IAI Dagger jets were soon dispatched over the South Atlantic to strike back at the British. *(Carlos Ay)*

BELGRANO

SINK THE
BELGRANO

Naval Action in the South Atlantic

Commander Chris Wreford-Brown, the skipper of HMS *Conqueror*, watched alone through a periscope as the torpedoes he had ordered to be fired at the ARA *General Belgrano,* closed on their target. The attack on the 600ft Argentine cruiser, a US vessel used during World War Two, killed 323 of the ship's crew.

In his log, released by the British Ministry of Defence in 2012, Wreford-Brown wrote: "Orange fireball seen just aft of the centre of target, in line with the aft mast, shortly after the first explosion was heard. Second explosion heard about five seconds later after. I think I saw a spurt of water aft, but it may have been smoke from the first. Third explosion heard but not seen — I was not looking!"

At 4.25pm that day he had written: "Traffic now received. COR177 [message from submarine command in Northwood] gives me permission to attack."

An entry at 6.56pm reads "FIRE Order of firing [torpedo tubes] 6, 1, 2".

The dry entries in Wreford-Brown's log put to rest some of the controversy surround the sinking of the Argentine cruiser. For years Margaret Thatcher had been criticised for

ordering the attack on the warship outside the 200nm total exclusion zone. Hector Bonzo, the cruiser's captain, was later quoted as describing the attack as a legitimate act of war and he recognised his ship was at risk as soon as the shooting war began on May 1.

The countdown to the sinking of the ARA *General Belgrano* began in the early morning of May 1, as reports of the first British air strikes on Port Stanley reached the Junta in Buenos Aires. When reports were received of British warships off the Falklands it appeared that a landing was underway. At the same time as the Argentine air force was ordered to strike at the British task group, the Argentine navy was also instructed to attack. Two naval task groups, including the aircraft carrier, ARA *Veinticinco de Mayo,* were ordered to move around the northern edge of the Falklands exclusion zone, supported by the only working submarine, to strike at the British aircraft carriers. At the same time, the ARA *General Belgrano* and her group of destroyers were to skirt around the southern edge of the exclusion zone before attacking.

Britain's GCHQ signals intelligence organisation intercepted and decoded the Junta's commands to their fleet. Soon, Rear Admiral Sandy

Woodward was alerted to the looming threat. Royal Navy nuclear attack submarines were already moving to intercept the Argentine task groups in the run up to May 1 strikes on Port Stanley. HMS *Conqueror* had picked up the *General Belgrano* on that day but HMS *Splendid* had yet to find the Argentine carrier.

During the air action around Port Stanley, the Argentine fleet continued to steam east with the intention of launching an air strike on the British carriers and engaging other warships with ship-launched Exocet missiles. However, the Argentine task group commander, Rear Admiral Jorge Allara, had not yet located the British carriers. During May 1 he launched Tracker maritime patrol aircraft to search for their targets using newly installed electronic equipment to detect British radar emissions. Two planes returned to the carrier with information about the British fleet. A third Tracker was launched after dark to update the intelligence, but this aircraft was detected by a Sea Harrier patrolling around the British task force. It pursued the Tracker and soon picked up the distinctive radar signals from an Argentine Type 42 destroyer. Now both the British and Argentine fleet commanders knew their opponent's locations. Admiral Allara ordered his carrier group to reverse course to escape.

By the evening of May 1, the Junta had worked out that they had been tricked and there was no British landing on the Falklands. There was no need launch an immediate attack, so the *General Belgrano* was also ordered to head back towards the Argentine coast to remain in formation with the carrier group. Both groups of warships were ordered to be ready to re-engage should the British attempt another landing. On the ARA *Veinticinco de Mayo,* Admiral Allara still thought there was an opportunity to attack so he turned his task group around and headed east so the carrier would be within range of the British fleet at dawn. Unusually low winds saved the British. As the carrier arrived on station, the wind dropped, and it proved impossible to launch her eight Skyhawks with a full fuel and bomb load. She turned around and headed back towards Argentina.

Admiral Woodward was unaware of the Argentine fleet movements during the early hours of May 2. He was working out his options to neutralise the threats to his fleet. HMS *Conqueror* still had the *General Belgrano* in her sights but did not yet have permission to engage the ship. The submarine was also not under Woodward's command but was controlled directly from the task force

The iconic image of the ARA *General Belgrano* sinking on the May 2, 1982 taken by an Argentine navy officer from a life raft. *(Martín Sgut)*

headquarters at Northwood by Vice Admiral Peter Herbert, the Flag Officer Submarines. This was normally a long, drawn-out process but Woodward did not think he had time to go through this. Instead, he issued a direct order to Wreford-Brown to attack the Argentine ship. Woodward was fully aware that the satellite radio message would be routed through Herbert's office, and he would intercept the command. This, hopefully, would kick-start Hebert and his boss, Admiral Fieldhouse, to rapidly get the War Cabinet into agreeing to the order for *Conqueror* to attack the cruiser.

Woodward's move had the desired effect and by mid-morning on May 2, Fieldhouse was heading to the Prime Minister's country residence, Chequers, to brief the War Cabinet. There was little discussion and Margaret Thatcher, and her minister approved the new Rules of Engagement, or ROE, for Wreford-Brown. It took a few hours for the message to be successfully passed to HMS *Conqueror*, which needed to break off trailing the *General Belgrano* to re-establish radio contact with the satellite and download his new orders. At the first attempt the message was garbled, and a second attempt had to be made to re-establish communications. Wreford-Brown sent his own update back to Northwood, reporting that the Argentine cruiser had changed course and was now heading west, away from the Falklands. Admiral Herbert did not think it changed the situation and did not countermand Wreford-Brown's new orders or pass this new information up to Fieldhouse.

In the South Atlantic, Wreford-Brown now moved to attack. It took some time to re-acquire the Argentine cruiser and her escorts. He had to manoeuvre his submarine to within 1,400 yards of his target to fire three Mark 8 torpedoes. These were World War Two era, unguided weapons but they were far more reliable that the wire-guided Tigerfish torpedoes that were also in HMS *Conqueror*'s weapons store.

Two of the three torpedoes hit ARA *General Belgrano*. One hit amidships and exploded in

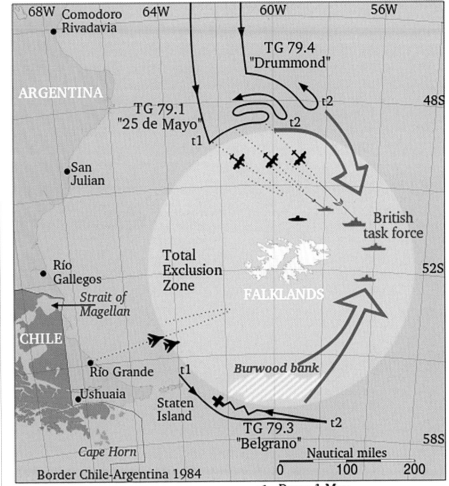

1 May Tracker recce flights
Expected Argentine attack
Tracker-Fleet radar contact
Aborted Exocet attack
"ARA San Luis" fires torpedoes against "HMS Exeter"

t1 Dawn 1 May
t2 2 May 5:00
✖ "ARA Belgrano" sunk 2 May 17:57
1982: Administered by Chile claimed by Argentina

British and Argentine naval forces manoeuvred for advantage on May 1-2, 1982. *(Keysanger)*

The ARA *Veinticinco de Mayo* tried to launch her A-4 Skyhawk jets to attack the British task group on the morning of May 2, but low winds prevented the aircraft taking off. *(Argentine Navy)*

The Churchill-class nuclear-powered attack submarine HMS *Conqueror* returns to her base at Faslane after her war cruise to the South Atlantic, flying a Jolly Roger to mark a successful operational mission. The display of the pirate flag is a tradition of the Royal Navy Submarine Service dating back to World War Two. *(DPL)*

South Atlantic Military Theatre Operations, May 1-2, 1982
Commander: Vice Admiral Juan Lombardo
Puerto Belgrano Naval Base, Buenos Aires Province

Task Group 79.1

Commander: Rear Admiral Jorge Allara

ARA *Veinticinco de Mayo* (Colossus-class aircraft carrier) (8 x A-4Q Skyhawk, 5 x S-2E Trackers, 3 x Sea King helicopters)

ARA *Santísima Trinidad* (Argentine-built Type 42 destroyer (1 x Lynx HAS.23 helicopter)

ARA *Punta Médanos* (fleet tanker)

Task Group 79.3

Commander: Captain Héctor Bonzo

ARA *General Belgrano* (Brooklyn-class cruiser) (1 x Alouette helicopter)

ARA *Hipólito Bouchard* (Allen M. Sumner-class destroyer)

ARA *Piedra Buena* (Allen M. Sumner-class destroyer)

ARA *Punta Delgada* (fleet tanker)

Task Group 79.4

Commander: Captain Juan Calmon

ARA *Granville* (Drummond-class corvette)

ARA *Drummond* (Drummond-class corvette)

ARA *Guerrico* (corvette)

Submarine Force

ARA *San Luis* (Type 209 submarine)

The British built Type 42 Destroyer ARA *Hércules* was escorting the ARA *Veinticinco de Mayo* on the morning of May 2. *(Argentine Navy)*

The corvette ARA *Drummond* was part of the northern pincer movement against the British naval task group. *(Mauricio V. Genta)*

HMS *Conqueror*	
Churchill-class submarine	
Builder	Cammell Laird, Birkenhead
Laid down	December 5, 1967
Launched	August 28, 1969
Commissioned	November 9, 1971
Displacement	4,900 tonnes
Length	86.9m (285ft)
Beam	10.1m (33ft)
Speed	28kts (52km/h) (submerged)
Complement	103
Armament	6 × 533 mm tubes capable of firing Mark 8 torpedoes, Tigerfish torpedoes

The ARA *General Belgrano* survived the Japanese attack on Pearl Harbor as the USS *Phoenix* and was sold to Argentina in 1951. *(Argentine Navy)*

ARA *General Belgrano*	
(ex USS *Phoenix*)	
Brooklyn-class light cruiser	
Laid down	April 25, 1935
Acquired by Argentina	1951
Displacement	12,242 tons
Length	185.4m (608.3ft)
Beam	18.8m (61.8ft)
Speed	60.2 km/h (32.5kts)
Complement	1,138 officers and sailors
Armament	15 × 6in (150mm), 8 × 5in (130mm) AA, 40mm and 20mm anti-aircraft guns, two British Sea Cat missile AA systems (added 1968)
Aircraft carried	1 x Aérospatiale Alouette III

the engine compartment. The ship quickly started to take on water. The crew had left open many of the ship's watertight doors and within minutes smoke, flames and water were engulfing the ship. Captain Bonzo ordered his crew to abandon ship. Many of the crew then spent two days afloat in life rafts as Argentine and Chilean rescue ships scoured the South Atlantic looking for survivors. In the end, 772 of her 1,042 crew were rescued.

In the aftermath of the attack the cruiser's escorts started to hunt for HMS *Conqueror,* dropping depth charges at random. Wreford-Brown ordered his submarine to dive deep to evade his pursuers and find a safe location to re-establish communications with Northwood to report his successful attack.

After the war it was claimed that Margaret Thatcher had deliberately ordered the sinking of the cruiser to scupper a peace plan devised by the Peruvian government. It subsequently emerged that details of the peace plan had not yet been passed to the War Cabinet in London by the Foreign Secretary, Francis Pym, who was in the United States. The Junta in Buenos Aires had not even discussed the plan by the time the ARA *General Belgrano* was attacked.

When news of the ship's sinking arrived, the Junta ordered all its ships to withdraw back into coastal waters where they would be safe from British submarines. They remained there for the rest of the war. Wreford-Brown's attack had given the Royal Navy mastery of South Atlantic.

HMS *Sheffield* was the first British warship to be lost to enemy action since World War Two. *(DPL)*

EXOCET ATTACK ON
HMS *SHEFFIELD*

Argentina Strikes Back at the British Task Group

HMS *Sheffield* was the first major British warship to be lost to enemy action since World War Two. The sense of shock in the Royal Navy, British government, media, and public after news was released of her fate late on May 4 was palpable. The Argentine military had graphically demonstrated that they had the weapons and wherewithal to use them to deadly effect. The campaign to recapture the Falklands was clearly not going to be a one-sided walkover.

The first two days of combat around and over the Falkland Islands had gone largely Britain's way but the commanders and sailors in the task group were convinced that the Argentines had not yet committed their best weapons or units to action. Since the major Argentine forays on May 1, they had pulled their air and naval forces back to their home waters and bases, leaving the British free to operate in the 200nm total exclusion zone. Rear Admiral Sandy Woodward was now focusing on tightening the air and naval embargo around the islands to prevent supplies and reinforcements reaching the Argentine garrison. At the same time, he wanted to sail his own ships close enough to the Falklands to launch helicopters to drop off Special Air Service and Special Boat Squadron reconnaissance teams to build an accurate intelligence picture for the planners preparing the British landing.

The British task group assumed station astride the eastern fringe of the exclusion zone, which was close enough to the Falklands to allow night time dashes by helicopters to land the covert surveillance teams and for Sea Harriers to patrol around Port Stanley to deter daytime air traffic using the airport. It also meant there was plenty of sea room for the task group to manoeuvre in and prevent the Argentine air force using the islands to mask their operations.

Admiral Woodward deployed his ships in layers to provide defence in depth against air attack. The outer crust of his defence was a picket line of his three Type 42 air defence destroyers – running north to south, HMS *Coventry*, HMS *Glasgow*, and HMS *Sheffield*. They had long range radar to give early warning of Argentine air and missile attacks, electronic surveillance equipment to detect and identify hostile radars, and the Sea Dart air defence missile. Sea Dart was designed to engage Russian bombers at medium and

A French made Exocet missile successfully penetrated the British task group's defences to hit HMS *Sheffield*. *(DPL)*

An Argentine naval aviation P-2 Neptune flew ahead of two Super Étendard strike jets to find the British task group. *(Argentine Navy)*

high altitude out to 40nm range. These were some of the newest ships in the Royal Navy, but their weapons and radars had been dogged by technical problems for years although the Ministry of Defence claimed all the 'bugs and gremlins' in their computer systems had been sorted out by 1982.

Behind this picket line of Type 42s were the two carriers, HMS *Hermes* and HMS *Invincible,* and they were each protected by one of the latest Type 22 frigates armed with the short range Sea Wolf air defence missiles. The frigates were nicknamed 'goalkeepers' because they were considered the carriers' last line of defence.

HMS *Sheffield* was the first Type 42 air defence destroyer when she entered service in 1975. Her first captain was Sandy Woodward, who in May 1982 was commander of the British naval task group. *(US Navy)*

The Super Étendard was the most modern strike aircraft in Argentine naval aviation service after being delivered from France between August and November 1981. *(Argentine Navy)*

Sea Harriers flew combat air patrols around the fleet but there were not enough planes and pilots to keep this up 24/7 so there were long periods when none of the jets were airborne.

Behind the carriers were the supply ships and tankers that were needed to keep the task group fighting. They were protected by the ageing County-class destroyers and older frigates.

Late on the morning of May 4, the British task group was in its operational area waiting for events to unfold. There were intermittent radar contacts, and many were dismissed as false alarms by jumpy radar operators and their controllers. The air defence of the task group was being co-ordinated by the battle staff in the operations room of HMS *Invincible*.

Since the sinking of the ARA *General Belgrano* the Argentine navy had been preparing to strike back. That task fell to its naval aviation, or Comando de Aviación Naval (COAN), detachment at Rio Grande air base in the far south of the country. A P-2 Neptune maritime patrol aircraft launched from the base on the morning of May 4. It was followed by a pair of Super Étendard jets of the 2nd Fighter and Attack Squadron and an air force C-130 Hercules refuelling tanker. The Neptune found the British fleet and passed on their co-ordinates to the Super Étendards. After taking on extra fuel from the tanker, the two jets dropped down to low level to pass around the southern coast of the Falklands to line up for their attack.

The jets were armed with two of Argentina's five Exocet missiles. They had only been delivered to the country earlier in the year. French technicians had not yet completed the integration of the missiles onto the Super Étendards at the beginning of April and they left for home after the European Community imposed its arms embargo on Argentina. The Argentine navy had to complete the integration work itself.

As they made their final approach, the jets had to momentarily pop-up to allow the Exocet's internal radar to acquire their targets. Then they dropped down to low level again and released the two weapons, before turning for home. This took a matter of minutes to execute, and the British fleet would have even less time to react. The full details of what happened in those vital minutes were only revealed in full in 2000 when the Ministry of Defence released the board of inquiry report into the incident.

The first British ship to react was HMS *Glasgow*. Its electronic warfare operators picked up the emission of the Exocet's radar as they popped up to acquire their target. It called out a warning over the task group radio net. The ships went to action stations to be ready for the incoming missiles and orders were issued to start firing chaff to decoy the weapons. Controllers in HMS *Invincible* could not see the radar signal themselves and were sceptical, saying it was just a false alarm. There had already been several over the previous four days. Nothing to worry about, they said.

On HMS *Sheffield*, the nearest British ship to the threat, their own electronic warning equipment was offline because a satellite communications system that used the same frequencies was transmitting. Her commanding officer, Captain Sam Salt, was off duty in his cabin and the next most senior officers who should have been in the operations room co-ordinating the defence of the ship were elsewhere.

Seconds after the missiles were released, HMS *Glasgow* picked them up on radar and the crew started to issue desperate radio warnings to the task group. On HMS *Invincible*, the warnings were still not taken seriously, and Sea Harriers were not launched to intercept the Super Étendards.

There was little sign of reaction on HMS *Sheffield*. The first warnings were only raised when officers on the ship's bridge saw the smoke trails from a missile on the horizon. They shouted a warning over the ship's public address system, calling on the crew to 'hit the deck'. It was too little, too late. No chaff was fired and seconds later the missile hit square amidships, just below the bridge. There is still uncertainty about whether the missile's warhead actually exploded but the impact of the weapon was enough the shake the ship. As the weapon penetrated through the hull it ripped apart several compartments, cutting power and water lines as well as starting fires as it went. Within seconds the ship was full of acrid smoke and pandemonium ensued.

Air-to-air refuelling from an Argentine air force KC-130 tanker aircraft was essential to allowing the Super Étendards to reach their missile launch position to the southeast of the Falkland Islands. *(Martín Otero)*

Dassault-Breguet Super Étendard	
Crew	1
Length	14.31m (46ft 11in)
Wingspan	9.6m (31ft 6in)
Max take-off weight	12,000kg (26,455lb)
Maximum speed	1,205km/h (749mph, 651kts)
Range	1,820km (1,130m, 980nm)
Combat range	850km (530 miles, 460nm)
Armament	2 × 30 mm (1.18 in) DEFA 552 cannons; 4 × Matra SNEB 68 mm rocket pods; 1 × AM-39 Exocet Anti-shipping missile or 2 × Matra Magic Air-to-air missile; Conventional unguided or laser-guided bombs, provision for 'buddy' air refuelling pod

HMS *Sheffield* Type 42 destroyer	
Builder	Vickers Shipbuilding and Engineering Ltd, Barrow
Laid down	January 15, 1970
Launched	June 10, 1971
Commissioned	February 16, 1975
Displacement	4,820 tonnes
Length	125m (410ft 1in)
Beam	14.3m (46ft 11in)
Speed	56km/h (30kts)
Complement	21 officers and 249 ratings
Armament	2 × Sea Dart surface-to-air missile launchers, 1 × 4.5-inch (114 mm) Mk.8 gun
Aircraft carried	1 × Lynx HAS1

The centre of the ship was soon an inferno, forcing Captain Salt and his senior officers to vacate the bridge and operations room. Damage control teams fought a losing battle to keep fire away from the ship's fuel tanks and Sea Dart missile magazines. The frigates HMS *Arrow* and HMS *Yarmouth* closed to the destroyer to take off wounded and help fight the fires. Helicopters from HMS *Hermes* arrived to shuttle the wounded to safety.

After a few hours, Captain Salt realised his vessel was doomed and gave the order to abandon ship. Out of a crew of 281, 20 were dead and 26 injured, many of whom were seriously burned. Fire now consumed the ship, and she was left to burn herself out. HMS *Yarmouth*

eventually took the hulk under tow to avoid giving the Argentines the chance to seize her but on May 10 water surged through the hole in the hull, causing the ship to roll over and sink.

When Woodward met Salt on the deck of HMS *Hermes* after flying off his ship, the task group commander reportedly was less than sympathetic, commenting: "I suspect someone's been bloody careless." Several of HMS *Sheffield*'s crew were subsequently criticised by the board of inquiry. The task group commander, Admiral Sir John Fieldhouse, declined to take disciplinary action against the officers involved, to "avoid creating the wrong atmosphere in the press and souring the general euphoria" recalled Woodward after the war.

HMS *Arrow* pulled alongside HMS *Sheffield* to help fight the fires on the ship and evacuate her wounded crewmen. *(MOD)*

Wideawake airfield on Ascension Island became the busiest airport on the planet during April and May 1982. *(MOD, via David Oliver)*

CLEARING THE DECKS
FOR ACTION

The British Build-up

In the aftermath of the first air and naval clashes in the South Atlantic, the British task group commander, Rear Admiral Sandy Woodward, moved to tighten the blockade around the Falkland Islands to prevent reinforcements and supplies reaching the Argentine garrison.

The Argentine Junta realised that the British were not imminently about to launch their main landing, so orders were issued to the air force and navy to conserve their fighting power until

A Sea King cross-decks supplies onto the liner *Canberra*. *(DPL)*

Paratroopers run around the deck of the liner *Canberra* to keep fit on the cruise to the South Atlantic. *(DPL)*

the crucial moment in the campaign arrived. This meant that Woodward's task group was not really seriously challenged again until later in May.

The Argentine navy was effectively bottled up in port or inside the country's 12-mile territorial waters by the presence of British nuclear-powered attack submarines patrolling the South Atlantic. However, the A-4Q Skyhawk strike jets and S-2E Tracker maritime patrol aircraft were disembarked from the ARA *Veinticinco de Mayo* and sent to Rio Grande airbase in the far south of Argentina to prepare to strike at the British fleet.

Considerable effort was put in to finding the British task group to give some warning of when the amphibious landing would take place. An improvised network of trawlers and merchant vessels was mobilised to report on British naval movements across the South Atlantic, from the Argentine coast up to Ascension Island and out towards South Africa. It was hoped that the British would not attack these civilian vessels, even within the 200 mile exclusion zone around the Falklands. The Argentine air force also recruited a force of civilian pilots, the so-called

Escuadrón Fénix, to fly surveillance missions in their own aircraft to try to augment the work of the navy maritime patrol aircraft. The British signals intelligence agency GCHQ picked up the traffic from these vessels and aircraft. They alerted Woodward to the threat they posed.

On May 9, one of these vessels, the commandeered trawler, *Narwal,* was detected by British warships southeast of Port Stanley. A Sea Harrier was sent to identify the ship and Woodward ordered the jet to drop bombs to immobilise it and then called for a Special Boat Squadron (SBS) boarding party to be landed aboard by helicopter. The SBS assault team secured the ship and captured an Argentine naval intelligence officer and his code books. Hours later the ship sank as a result of the damage from one of the bombs.

During this incident, an Argentine Coast Guard Puma helicopter was launched from Port Stanley to try to find the missing ship. It was detected by HMS *Coventry,* which was leading a group of British ships to bombard Port Stanley airport and was engaged with a Sea Dart surface-to-air missile. The helicopter was destroyed, and its three crew killed in the first-ever shooting down of an enemy aircraft by a Royal Navy guided missile.

The daily sorties by British ships to bombard Port Stanley airport were increasingly irritating Argentine commanders and on May 12 they decided to strike back. Three flights, each of four air force A-4B Skyhawks, were

A Sea Harrier and Wessex helicopter prepare to land on the *Atlantic Conveyor* as she is loaded for her one way cruise to the Falklands. *(DPL)*

launched from the mainland to strike at HMS *Glasgow* and *HMS Brilliant* off Port Stanley.

They made their final approach at low level over the Falkland Islands. The British ships had only a few minutes to react. HMS *Glasgow* tried to engage the first wave of jets with her long range Sea Dart, but salt water corrosion prevented the launcher mechanism from working. The ship then began to engage the jets with her 4.5-inch

forward cannon and crew members were on the upper decks firing machine guns at them. Fortunately, HMS *Brilliant*'s short range Sea Wolf surface-to-air missile system was up to the job and shot down two of the incoming jets. The third tried to turn away but the pilot flew into the sea. This left only one jet to drop its bombs. They all missed.

Within minutes the second wave moved to attack. HMS *Glasgow*'s Sea Dart was still not working and now her 4.5 inch cannon jammed. It was put back into action, but the shell fire was now confusing HMS *Brilliant*'s Sea Wolf radar, and the missiles could not lock on. The Argentine jets got through and dropped their bombs. Most missed but one hit *Glasgow* amidships. The bomb failed to explode and passed straight through the ship, leaving two large holes in her hull. The machine gun fire from the ship's crew had damaged the jet that dropped that bomb. As it limped home the aircraft was shot down by accident by Argentine gunners at Goose Green. The last flight of Skyhawks did not engage and returned to base without dropping their ordnance.

HMS *Glasgow* was soon patched up and back in action, but the events of May 12 indicated that the Royal Navy's missile defences might not be as effective as originally thought.

USAF C-141 Starlifter aircraft joined the airlift to Wideawake airfield on Ascension Island to deliver secret supplies from the Pentagon's stockpiles. *(Bob Shackleton)*

Royal Navy Sea King HAS5 anti-submarine helicopters flew constant patrols around the task group. Two were lost when they ditched after suffering technical problems. Their crews were successfully rescued. *(DPL)*

Argentine Pucara light attack aircraft were the target of the SAS raid on Pebble Island. *(DPL)*

PEBBLE ISLAND RAID

Neutralising an Argentine Airbase

By mid-May, Rear Admiral Sandy Woodward and his amphibious planners were beginning to focus on the San Carlos region as the most promising landing site to put ashore the Royal Marines of 3 Commando Brigade.

Special Air Service (SAS) and Special Boat Service (SBS) reconnaissance teams had been landed on the islands to gather intelligence and build up a detailed picture of Argentine deployments and the conditions of potential landing beaches. The SAS and SBS men established small observation posts on hillsides overlooking their targets and lay undiscovered for days on end. They watched what was happening and built up a detailed picture of Argentine defences. SBS troopers also made night time forays from

HMS *Hermes* made a night-time dash around the north of the Falkland Islands to launch and recover Sea King helicopters carry the SAS raiding team to Pebble Island. *(MOD)*

their hides to inspect beaches and assess if they were suitable to put troops ashore on.

To successfully put ashore at San Carlos, Woodward needed to ensure that no sea mines had been planted in Falkland Sound that

separated the islands of East and West Falkland. At that time, the British task group had no specialist mine-hunting vessels so the only way to find out for sure was to send a warship to sail through Falkland Sound. The Type 21 frigate,

HMS *Alacrity,* was given the job and she made her perilous journey on the night of May10-11. During her uneventful passage, the warship detected and engaged a 3,000 ton Argentine navy supply ship, the ARA *Isla de los Estados,* with her 4.5-inch main armament. The ship was loaded with ammunition and aviation fuel for the garrison on West Falkland and it exploded, creating a massive fireball, killing all but two of the 22 crew.

When *Alacrity* emerged from the north end of Falkland Sound, she joined up with HMS *Arrow* to make the passage back to the main task group. During this manoeuvre, the Argentine Type 209 submarine ARA *San Lois* engaged the two ships. She attempted to fire two guided torpedoes, but one never left the boat and the other suffered a guidance system failure. This was the last time the submarine would try to engage British warships.

Intelligence was building during early May that there were few Argentine forces based in the San Carlos region. The biggest threat was from a forward airfield on Pebble Island, near the northern entrance to Falkland Sound, where Argentine air force IA58 Pucara and navy T-34C Mentor light strike aircraft were based. Although not supersonic jets, these aircraft could wreak havoc if they managed to strafe or bomb poorly armed transport ships and landing craft.

Admiral Woodward gave the job of neutralising the threat to the SAS. A reconnaissance team was landed on East Falkland by helicopter and then made a crossing onto the island in a small boat. HMS *Hermes* made a night-time dash toward the Falklands on the night of May 14 to launch two Sea King HC4s carrying a 45 strong assault team from the SAS's D Squadron. They landed on Pebble Island in a gale and then marched five kilometres in darkness to the grass airfield.

The terrible weather allowed SAS demolition experts to infiltrate the airfield undetected

SAS troops cross-deck from HMS *Hermes* to HMS *Fearless* after the Pebble Island raid. *(DPL)*

and plant explosives on the aircraft. Once the charges were detonated, HMS *Glamorgan* started to bombard the airfield. The SAS troops opened up on the Argentine garrison to add to the destruction. They then broke contact and retreated to be picked up by helicopters for the return to HMS *Hermes.*

Once dawn broke the Argentine airmen found that their six Pucaras and four Mentors, as well as a Skyvan light transport aircraft

were badly damaged. The grass strip had been cratered. Ammunition and fuel dumps were also ablaze. This was a text-book special forces raiding operation that harked back to the early days of SAS in World War Two when the elite force had played havoc by striking at German airfields in North Africa. The airfield was effectively out of action, opening the way for the main British landing force to safely move down Falkland Sound to San Carlos.

The Argentine garrison remained on Pebble Island until end of the war. Naval aviation personnel were evacuated back to the mainland by two Sea King helicopters on June 1. (Argentine navy/Rescate-Borbón) *(DPL)*

STOP TAXIWAY AHEAD

The RAF's 51 Squadron dispatched Nimrod R1 XW644 to Chile to fly electronic intelligence gathering missions around the southern coast of Argentine. *(John Visanich)*

COVERT OPs

Neutralising the Exocet Threat

Senior Royal Air Force officers were acutely aware that their Royal Navy comrades were sailing towards the Falklands with no land-based air support, particularly any means to provide the task group with early warning of Argentine air attack. One solution to this key vulnerability was to call in some favours with Argentina's neighbour and sworn enemy, Chile.

In April 1982, a Spanish speaking RAF officer, Wing Commander Sydney Edwards, was dispatched to the Chilean capital, Santiago to establish links with President Augusto Pinochet's government and then function as a liaison with the Chilean air force. As a down-payment, a Royal Air Force Hercules delivered six surplus Hawker Hunter jets to the Chileans. Pinochet was happy to help make sure Argentina did not win the Falklands war, but he wanted to shield his country's involvement from prying eyes. There could be no trail back to Chile.

Edwards set up a series of covert operations involving British personnel and aircraft collaborating with the Chileans. First on the ground were a team of Special Air Service (SAS) communications experts, equipped with satellite radios, who were allowed to set up a cell in the Chilean air defence headquarters to pass on information about the movements of any Argentine aircraft detected by Pinochet's radar network.

To expand the radar coverage of southern Argentina, a RAF Marconi T259 radar with crew was flown by an RAF C-130, disguised with Chilean air force markings, to Balmaceda airport high in the Andes. From there it could monitor air traffic at the Argentine Comodoro Rivadara airbase. The mission was codenamed *Operation Fingent*.

The British wanted to base Nimrod MR2 maritime patrol and Nimrod R1 signals intelligence aircraft in Chile so they could protect the task group, but the Chileans did not want the distinctive aircraft at any of their mainland airbases in case Argentine spies spotted them. A compromise was devised in which a Nimrod R1 was based on San Felix Island in the South Pacific. On missions it flew to the Chilean airbase at Conception under cover of darkness to give it the range to hook around the tip of South America and begin its missions to monitor Argentine radar emissions and radio traffic. A Chilean officer would board the aircraft at Conception for this part of each mission.

Six missions were flown under the auspices of *Operation ACME* from May 5 to May 17 and were credited with picking up valuable intelligence on Argentine air and naval activity. The RAF were keen to add to the intelligence gathering effort by deploying two high flying Canberra PR9

An RAF S259 radar and its crew was secretly flown to Chile to monitor Argentine air operations. *(Marconi Radar History)*

reconnaissance jets to Chile to allow them take high resolution photographs of Argentine air and naval bases. A deal was struck in which the British would 'give' the Chileans the aircraft and then send RAF pilots and ground crew to train local crews. The Canberras of *Operation Folklore* got as far as the British airbase in Belize in central America when on May 18 the Chileans got cold feet after a Royal Navy Sea King HC4 helicopter had landed unannounced in southern Chile.

The sinking of HMS *Sheffield* on May 4 threatened to derail the whole British campaign to recapture the Falklands, so the SAS was asked to rapidly plan a strike at the Argentine airfield where the Exocet missile-armed jets were based.

The idea was to land SAS teams at Rio Grande air base in a re-run of the Israeli Entebbe raid. Two RAF Hercules C1s, of the recently formed Special Forces Flight of 47 Squadron, were to land directly on the airbase's main runway and then the SAS were to fan out, destroying the Exocets and the Super Étendards as well as killing their pilots. To gather intelligence for *Operation Mikado*, a Sea King HC4 was launched from HMS *Invincible* to fly a small SAS surveillance team close to the Rio Grande airbase. This part of the mission was codenamed *Operation Plum Duff*. As it approached the Argentine coast, the Sea King's crew suspected they had been detected by radar and diverted towards neutral Chile. The SAS team were dropped off inside Argentina and they later walked to Chile. The Royal Navy crew destroyed their helicopter and gave themselves up to the Chilean authorities. Despite protests from senior SAS officers, *Mikado* was cancelled. The unintended consequence of the publicity was that the Chileans got cold feet about the Canberra deployment and the Nimrod R1 flights. Both were closed down with immediate effect.

These covert operations were shrouded in secrecy until the official history of the Falklands war was published in 2006 and top secret files were released under the 30 Year Rule concerning official records. One covert mission remains secret despite hints of it appearing in other official documents. *Operation Shutter* is believed to have involved the British Secret Intelligence Service, or MI6, sending operatives into Argentina to set up covert observation posts outside airbases.

An RAF C-130 Hercules was repainted in Chilean air force colours to fly secret supply missions to the South American country, which was very hostile to Argentina. *(Mike Freer)*

A plan to secretly base Canberra PR9 photographic aircraft in Chile was scuppered by media coverage of a group of SAS troops entering the south of the country. After the war, the UK did supply Chile with Canberra PR9s. *(Aeroprints)*

Brazil supplied Argentina with EMB-111 Bandeirante light transport aircraft in May in a bid to fill its maritime patrol gap. *(Brazilian Air Force)*

Queen Elizabeth 2 cross decks troops of 5 Infantry Brigade off South Georgia. *(DPL)*

FORMING THE SECOND WAVE

Queen Elizabeth 2 *and 5 Infantry Brigade Sails*

The breaking down of peace talks in the first days of May led the British government to finally resolve to recapture the Falkland Islands. By this point British intelligence realised that the Argentine garrison on the islands was in excess of 10,000 troops. The 5,000 Royal Marines and Paratroopers that had sailed with the first wave of Royal Navy ships at the beginning of April were not considered sufficient to take on the Argentine garrison.

Senior British Army and Royal Marine officers wanted at least to have an equal number of troops available before attempting to join battle. An additional brigade was ordered to head south to boost the landing force into divisional strength, under the command of Royal Marines Major General Jeremy Moore.

The Aldershot-based 5 Infantry Brigade was given this task as it was nominally the British Army's rapid reaction force. It had been assigned this role by defence secretary John Nott in his infamous June 1981 defence review that had also cut the size of the Royal Navy. The move was controversial in the British Army because 5 Brigade had only been established in January 1982 and had not conducted any major training exercises to prepare it for its new role. Two of its best units, 2nd, and 3rd Battalions of

Civilian Ships Taken Up From Trade, or STUFT had helicopter landing pads and other modifications rapidly fitted before they sailed for the South Atlantic. *(DPL)*

The liner *Canberra* travelled to South Georgia to pick up 5 Infantry Brigade and then sailed for San Carlos Water. *(DPL)*

To avoid Argentine surveillance, the liner travelled south without using her radar and other navigation aids. Once in Cumberland Bay she laid anchor and her troops were cross decked into smaller vessels, including the *Canberra* and *Norland* to eventually make the dangerous run into San Carlos Water. The 70,000 ton liner was considered too much of a tempting target to risk bringing her within range of the Argentine air force. She returned home to Southampton on June 11.

the Parachute Regiment, had already sailed with 3 Commando Brigade so it had to be hurriedly reinforced with two battalions from Foot Guards regiments diverted from public duties guarding the Royal Palaces in London.

The long-established United Kingdom Mobile Force, based on 1 Infantry Brigade, was already trained, and equipped to reinforce NATO's northern flank but it was not considered for

Gurkha soldiers kept fit by running around the deck of *Queen Elizabeth 2*. *(DPL)*

political reasons. Consequently, 5 Brigade was sent to Wales for a training exercise and was ordered to be ready to sail by mid-May.

Transporting 5 Brigade and its equipment to the South Atlantic would require the mobilisation of more civilian vessels under a process known as Ships Taken Up From Trade, or STUFT. These requisitioned ships – passenger liners, car ferries, cargo ships, tankers, ocean-going trawlers, and salvage tugs - were pressed into Royal Navy service, with naval commanding officers assigned to work alongside their civilian captains. The ships' existing crews remained onboard under military command. By the time the war ended in June, more than 40 ships had been mobilised under the programme.

Naval communications, refuelling at sea equipment and military-standard helicopter landing pads were installed in record time at shipyards and naval dockyards.

The bulk of 5 Brigade sailed on the iconic Cunard liner, *Queen Elizabeth 2*, on May 12. Its vehicles, Gazelle AH1 and Scout AH1 light helicopters and other heavy equipment were transported on the roll-on, roll-off (Ro-Ro) ferries *Nordic Ferry* and *Baltic Ferry*. Additional Royal Navy Sea King and Wessex transport helicopters were loaded on the Ro-Ro container ship *Atlantic Causeway*. These helicopters were to move 5 Brigade and its equipment to Port Stanley.

The *Queen Elizabeth 2* raced to Ascension Island at full speed and picked up a naval escort before heading for South Georgia.

Merchant Ships Taken Up From Trade (STUFT) April 2 to June 14, 1982
Passenger Liners
Canberra
Uganda
Queen Elizabeth 2
Roll-on-Roll-off ferries
Elk
Baltic Ferry
Europic Ferry
Nordic Ferry
Norland
Rangatira
St Edmund
Tor Caledonia
Container / Cargo ships
Astronomer
Atlantic Conveyor
Atlantic Causeway
Contender Bezant
Myrmidon
Avelona Star
Geestport
Laertes
Lycaon
St Helena
Tankers
Alvega
Anco Charger
Balder London
British Avon
British Dart
British Esk
British Tamar
British Tay
British Test
British Trent
British Wye
Eburna
Fort Toronto
Scottish Eagle
Tugs / Repair / Support Ships
British Enterprise III
Iris
Irishman
Salvageman
Stena Inspector
Stena Seaspread
Wimpey Seahorse
Yorkshireman
Ocean Going Trawlers (re-named as warships to form 11th Minesweeper Counter Measures Squadron)
HMS *Cordella*
HMS *Farnella*
HMS *Junella*
HMS *Northella*
HMS *Pict*

Helicopters to support 5 Infantry Brigade were transported to the Falklands onboard the *Atlantic Causeway*. *(DPL)*

San Carlos Water seen from Sussex Mountain. It is a natural anchorage and was selected because it provided protection from South Atlantic storms and Argentine air attacks. *(DPL)*

MOVING INTO POSITION

The Amphibious Task Group Approaches San Carlos

A s the British gathered more intelligence on Argentine troop deployments and gained experience of operating around the Falklands, it was becoming clear that the best site to put a British landing force ashore was in San Carlos Water. This bay, which split into two smaller bays, provided shelter to allow landing craft to move troops and equipment ashore and was also surrounded by high hills, where anti-aircraft missile batteries could be sited. They also hid any ships in the bay from the view of aircraft or warships approaching across Falkland Sound.

There was an Argentine platoon of around 20 soldiers camped on the Fanning Head peninsula at the entrance to San Carlos Water. They had no heavy weapons, little shelter, and poor communications with their headquarters at Goose Green, 20 miles to the southeast. There were no metalled roads between Goose Green and the San Carlos region so there was little prospect of Argentine reinforcements arriving quickly once the alarm had been raised. The Argentine garrison had a reserve company of around 150 troops on Mount Kent, west of Port Stanley, on alert to move by helicopter but they would be no match for the 5,000 heavily armed Royal Marines and Paratroopers of 3 Commando Brigade.

By the second week of May, the naval task group commander, Rear Admiral Sandy Woodward, the amphibious task group commander, Commodore Mike Clapp, and the commander of 3 Commando Brigade, Brigadier Julian Thompson, were all agreed on the San Carlos

option, but the War Cabinet in London had still not signed off going ahead with the landing to re-capture the Falklands. Diplomacy was still playing out. Admiral Sir John Fieldhouse, the overall British task force commander told his subordinates in the South Atlantic to proceed with preparations until they heard otherwise.

The amphibious shipping and STUFT vessels carrying 3 Commando Brigade had sailed from Ascension Island in early May and rendezvoused with the naval task group on May 17 to the northeast of the Falklands. Final plans were set on May 18 when Woodward, Clapp, and Thompson met on HMS *Hermes*. The following day, the majority of troops on the liner *Canberra* were cross-decked onto smaller ships to reduce the risk of the operation being compromised

if the 'Big White Whale' was hit by an Argentine air attack. Landing craft and helicopters were used to shuttle the troops between the ships. Fortunately, a period of calm weather descended on the South Atlantic to allow this complex manoeuvre to be conducted relatively quickly. One of the Sea King helicopters carrying a contingent of Special Air Service (SAS) men from HMS *Hermes* to HMS *Fearless* crashed in the sea after a possible bird strike. Only nine of the 30 personnel on board survived.

During the evening of May 19, Woodward received final authorisation from Admiral Fieldhouse to proceed with *Operation Sutton*, as the landing was codenamed. The objective was to recapture the Falkland Islands and restore British administration. Woodward

The Roll-on Roll-off cargo ship, *Elk*, alongside HMS *Fearless* during the approach to San Carlos Water. *(DPL)*

was given the authority to select the actual day of the landing. He decided to go the following evening, with the troops set to land on the Falklands by dawn on May 21.

Thompson and Clapp wanted the amphibious shipping to approach the Falklands in daylight and make a dash to San Carlos just after dusk to give 3 Commando Brigade all night to go ashore under the cover of darkness. However, Woodward was fearful that this would expose the fully loaded amphibious shipping to Argentine air attack as they approached the Falklands in daylight, in open water. Consequently, he ordered the ships to approach under cover of darkness and for the first troops to go ashore at 0230hrs, giving them only a couple of hours of darkness to cover their landing. One destroyer and seven frigates would be positioned around San Carlos Water and Falkland Sound to defend the landing. The hills around the landing beaches would prevent the Argentines using their Exocet missiles to target one of the large ships carrying hundreds of troops. Hopefully, the bulk of the troops would be ashore long before

A new world distance record for an operational reconnaissance mission was set on May 15 by a Nimrod MR2 of 201 Squadron. It covered a distance of 13,357 kilometres (8,300 miles) over the South Atlantic in 19 hours 5 minutes, to find out if the Argentine fleet was at sea. *(DPL)*

the Argentines realised what was happening and could mobilise their air force to attack.

As the landing force approached the Falklands during evening of May 20, a frigate was dispatched to bombard Goose Green to convince the Argentine garrison that the British were coming ashore there. Forty SAS men joined the raid to make it more convincing. HMS *Antrim* dispatched its helicopter to land a Special Boat Squadron assault team to neutralise

the Argentine position on Fanning Head. The scene was now set for the largest British amphibious operation since World War Two.

Task Group 317.0 (Amphibious Task Group)
Commander: Commodore M.C. Clapp (HMS *Fearless*)

Landing Platform Docks
HMS *Fearless* with 4 LCU, 4 LCVP
HMS *Intrepid* with 4 LCU, 4 LCVP

County-class destroyer
HMS *Antrim*

Type 22 frigates
HMS *Brilliant*
HMS *Broadsword*

Type 21 frigate
HMS *Ardent*

Leander-class frigate
HMS *Argonaut*

Rothesay-class frigates
HMS *Plymouth*
HMS *Yarmouth*

Royal Fleet Auxiliary - Landing Ship Logistic
RFA *Sir Galahad*
RFA *Sir Geraint*
RFA *Sir Lancelot*
RFA *Sir Percivale*
RFA *Sir Tristram*

Royal Fleet Auxiliary - Supply ships
RFA *Fort Austin*
RFA *Stromness*

STUFT vessels
Canberra
Europic Ferry
Norland

Combat supplies were redistributed or cross decked around the amphibious group in the days before the landing at San Carlos Water. *(DPL)*

Six RAF Harrier GR3 jets were flown to HMS *Hermes* on May 18 from the *Atlantic Conveyor* to give the task group a dedicated ground attack capability for the first time. *(MOD)*

HMS *Fearless*	
Fearless-class landing platform dock	
Builder	Harland and Wolff, Belfast
Laid down	July 25, 1962
Launched	December 19, 1963
Commissioned	November 25, 1965
Decommissioned	March 18, 2002
Pennant	L10
Displacement	12,120 tons (full load)
Length	160m (520ft)
Beam	24m (80ft)
Complement	580
Armament	2 × 20 mm Cannon
Aircraft carried Up to five Sea King helicopters.	

Landing craft started to offload troops from the liner *Canberra* as soon as she arrived in San Carlos Water after dawn on May 21. *(DPL)*

D-DAY
AT SAN CARLOS WATER

The British Land on the Falklands

The morning of May 21, 1982 proved to be anticlimactic for the British. Rear Admiral Sandy Woodward's plan for the amphibious task group to approach San Carlos proved successful. Surprise was complete.

Special Boat Squadron (SBS) artillery observation officers started off the action by bringing down 4.5-inch naval gunfire from HMS *Antrim* on the Argentine position on Fanning Head in the early hours and nine of the Argentine contingent were killed or captured. The remaining troops fled into the night and had a long walk back to Argentine positions.

The assault ships, HMS *Fearless* and HMS *Intrepid,* were the first to enter San Carlos Water because their landing craft were vital to bring Paratroopers ashore from the *Norland*. As dawn was breaking the first soldiers of 2nd Battalion, The Parachute Regiment went ashore at the southern edge of San Carlos Water. Minutes later Royal Marines of 40 Commando were put ashore near San Carlos Settlement. They were subsequently joined by 45 Commando.

Other major units followed during the day, with 3rd Battalion, The Parachute Regiment and 42 Commando landing around Port San Carlos. Once the fighting troops were ashore, the landing craft and Mexeflote pontoons began to land 3 Commando Brigade's logistic equipment, stores, and ammunition.

Priority for helicopter lift was given to moving the Rapier surface-to-air missile firing units up on the hills around San Carlos Water. Great store was placed on these missiles creating an air defence umbrella that would allow the Royal Navy to pull its

Paratroopers come ashore at Port San Carlos on the morning of May 21. *(DPL)*

Royal Marines captured stragglers from the Argentine outpost on Fanning Point on the morning of May 21. *(DPL)*

Landings continued throughout May 21 as the British raced to get their troops ashore before the Argentine air force could launch a counter strike. *(DPL)*

frigates back out to sea, where they would be better able to defend themselves.

The Argentine troops at Fanning Head had been successfully neutralised by the SBS but the 42-strong garrison at San Carlos Settlement was not attacked. Its soldiers were still in position when the *Canberra* arrived off shore and they had a grandstand view of British troops being unloaded into landing craft at 8.10am. The Argentine commander decided to retreat but before doing so radioed his superior officer at Goose Green about what he had seen. The British had now lost the element of surprise.

As the Argentine troops withdrew, they engaged a low flying British Gazelle utility helicopter whose pilot that did not realise there were enemy troops in the area. The helicopter crashed in the bay and one crewman later died of his injuries. He was to be the only British fatality of *Operation Sutton*.

Later in the morning the news of the British landing had got back Port Stanley, where aerial reconnaissance was ordered to gather more information. A single navy Aeromacchi

After the combat troops came ashore in the first waves, support troops from the Commando Logistic Regiment began building stockpiles of supplies and ammunition. *(DPL)*

MB-339A light strike jet launched from Port Stanley just before 10am and hooked around the north of East Falkland at low level. The pilot turned into Falkland Sound and caught sight of HMS *Argonaut*, which was positioned to guard the entrance to San Carlos Water. He dived at the frigate and strafed her with cannons and rocket, before swinging east to overfly the British anchorage. During a daredevil low level pass, the pilot was able to count all the ships and note their types. Almost every British weapon on and around San Carlos Water opened fire on the lone jet but miraculously it was not hit. It landed safely back at Port Stanley and the pilot personally briefed the Argentine commander, Brigade General Mario Menéndez on what he had seen. Reports were dispatched back to the Argentine mainland, where the air force and navy was busy arming and preparing scores of jets to strike at the British fleet. The Battle of San Carlos, or Bomb Alley, as it was soon nicknamed, was about to begin.

Argentine jets pressed home their attacks at low level to try to avoid the wall of shells and missiles put up by the British fleet. Here a Dagger attack jet over flies HMS *Fearless*. *(Rick Jolly)*

FRIGATES Vs SKYHAWKS

Argentine Air Power Strikes Back

At their airbases in southern Argentina, the country's air force and navy pilots had been preparing for this day for almost two months. The Argentine pilots pressed home their low level strikes against the British ships with great bravery. Television news footage showed the Argentine jets appearing to weave through the masts of British ships as anti-aircraft shells exploded around them.

In the end, the bravery of the Argentine pilots would not change the course of the war. Poor planning, unserviceable aircraft, bad weather, bomb fuses that did not work, long distances, and a lack of precise intelligence all counted against the Argentines. It was the latter that was most crucial. Not knowing the types and exact locations of British ships in and around San Carlos Water meant only a fraction of Argentine bombs hit home. Even the bombs that were dropped did not actually do any serious damage to British ships. Crucially, no British amphibious or civilian

ships were hit while they were loaded with troops and supplies. No British soldiers or Royal Marines were killed by the Argentine air force on May 21.

Since the conflict, the records of the Argentine air units have been made public and independent analysts, including the authors Jeffrey Ethell, Alfred Price, Martin Middlebrook and John Shields, have been able to piece together the details of the Battle of San Carlos. Air battles are notoriously difficult to make sense of, with multiple observers getting confused about what they see. Pilots and anti aircraft gunners have always over-claimed kills in the heat of battle, and it was no different in the Falklands War.

The Argentine plan involved launching several waves of between 10 and 20 aircraft during the day in the hope of overwhelming British defences. After air-to-air refuelling en route to the Falklands, the Argentine jets would make their final approach at low level over West Falkland

British Blowpipe missile teams joined in the barrage whenever Argentine jets appeared over San Carlos Water. *(DPL)*

After ignoring the British amphibious shipping in San Carlos during their May 21 attacks, the Argentine air force began to target civilian vessels, including the liner *Canberra* during air raids on subsequent days. *(DPL)*

This set the scene for the rest of the day. Eleven more formations involving more than 60 Argentine jets were launched into action but just over half were able to make attack runs and dropped just 44 bombs. Out of them, only eight hit their targets and then only half of those exploded.

On the British ships the crews used every weapon to hand to fight back – 4.5-inch naval guns, 40mm Bofors guns, 20mm Oerlikon cannons and machine guns. The close proximity of the hills around the anchorage played havoc with the radar systems on the Sea Wolf missiles on the two Type 22 frigates and they shot down no enemy aircraft that day, despite a number of kill claims being made.

It fell to the Sea Harriers to inflict the most damage on the Argentine pilots, shooting down nine of their jets – five Skyhawks and four Daggers – during the day. Except in one incident when three Daggers were intercepted approaching Falkland Sound, all the Argentine aircraft were shot down as they escaped 'the box' after dropping their bombs.

before swooping across Falkland Sound on their final attack run. The Argentine jets were armed with iron, or dumb, bombs which meant they had to overfly their targets before releasing their weapons. To try to smooth the way to their targets, the pilots opened fire with their cannons. It required strong nerves and considerable skill to actually get a bomb on target.

To defend the anchorage, British frigates were positioned in Falkland Sound and in the entrance to San Carlos Water. This 'gun line' of warships was intended to pick off the enemy jets before they could get to the landing fleet. The operation was co-ordinated from the destroyer HMS *Antrim*, which also had control of Sea Harrier combat air patrols flying to the north and south of San Carlos. Navy planners called San Carlos Water and the north end of Falkland Sound 'the box' and all British Sea Harriers were banned from flying into it. This made it very simple for the anti-aircraft gunners on the fleet – if any jets flew into view, they were Argentine, and the British could let rip with no fear of hitting a friendly aircraft. British helicopters were ordered to rapidly land when an air raid was called to avoid getting caught in the hail of fire that would erupt from the fleet during air attacks. Fighter controllers on *Antrim* directed the Sea Harriers to intercept enemy aircraft heading towards the box or escaping after they had made their attack runs. HMS *Brilliant* took over this vital job after HMS *Antrim* was put out of action.

The Argentine air force was first into action late on the morning of May 21 when a formation of 12 Dagger aircraft made an appearance over Falkland Sound. Flights of three jets broke up to strike at HMS *Argonaut*, HMS *Broadsword*, HMS *Antrim* and HMS *Brilliant*. They managed to drop nine bombs but only one hit its target, HMS *Antrim*. The big destroyer was badly damaged by cannon fire from the jets and eventually had to take cover in San Carlos Water to conduct repairs. Other ships had close shaves as bombs exploded around them. The British surface-to-air missiles again proved temperamental with only one missile hitting a Dagger. The rest of the Argentine jets returned safely to base.

Great store was placed on the Rapier air defence missile system by the British, but the weapon proved a disappointment. *(DPL)*

British landing ships came under attack on May 24 with two being hit but the Argentine bombs did not explode. *(DPL)*

The Rothesay-class frigate HMS *Plymouth* joined the gun line in Falkland Sound to try to shoot down Argentine jets before they could reach amphibious shipping in San Carlos Water. *(DPL)*

This success came at a cost. HMS *Ardent* was lost after four bombs detonated on her. HMS *Antrim* and HMS *Argonaut* had unexploded bombs inside. And both HMS *Broadsword* and HMS *Brilliant* had been badly damaged by cannon fire.

The warships protecting the amphibious landing had taken a heavy pounding, but the Argentine pilots made a major tactical error in concentrating on attacking the 'gun line' in Falkland Sound. They allowed more than 3,000 troops to get ashore with over 1,000 tons of supplies. The British were firmly ashore on the Falklands and would not be expelled.

Bad weather in southern Argentina on May 22 meant less than 10 jets could get airborne to attack the British. None of them were able to find targets and drop their bombs. This gave the British time to land more troops and supplies,

Better weather the following day allowed 34 Argentine jets to be launched against San Carlos. However, the same problems continued to bedevil the attack pilots and only four of their formations managed to release their bombs. Three Daggers made an ineffective bombing run on British troops at San Carlos. HMS *Antelope* was the focus of the attack, and she was hit by two bombs which did not immediately explode. The ship broke its back and sank when one of the bombs went off later. One of the attacking Skyhawks hit the warship's mast before being caught by fire from multiple directions. Sea Wolf, Sea Cat and Blowpipe missile operators all claimed to have shot down the jet. The Sea Harriers shot down a Dagger over Pebble Island later in the afternoon.

As these attacks were underway, the Argentine navy launched two of its Super Étendards loaded with two of their remaining three Exocet missiles. The planes returned to base after being unable to find a target.

On May 23, the Argentine pilots returned to San Carlos again but in smaller numbers, with only 24 jets being launched into action. The intensity of the previous day's action

was taking its toll. At least 10 of the 70 or so strike jets in southern Argentina had been lost and several others had been damaged. Maintenance crews were struggling to repair them and find spares to fix a long list of technical faults on the rest of the fleet.

After three days of concentrating their efforts on the warships in the gun line out in Falkland Sound, the strikes on May 24 were focused on landing ships inside San Carlos Water. The landing ships RFA *Sir Bedivere*, RFA *Sir Galahad* and RFA *Sir Lancelot* were hit with four bombs that failed to explode. Other British ships were strafed by the Argentine jets. Despite the change, the new tactics had little impact - the British landing ships were empty after unloading most of their troops and cargo.

The Royal Artillery Rapier and Blowpipe missile batteries were now fully operational around San Carlos and one Skyhawk was shot down, although again multiple ships and units claimed the kill. The wall of fire put up by British damaged many of the Argentine aircraft.

This day also saw the British try a new tactic in a bid to improve their radar coverage of incoming Argentine jets so the Sea Harriers could be vectored to intercept them before they reached San Carlos Water. A Type 45 destroyer was moved to patrol just to the north of Pebble Island. This would allow its long range radar to 'see' around West Falkland and give vital early warning to the Sea Harrier combat air patrols. A Type 22 frigate, HMS *Broadsword,* was sent to provide close protection to HMS *Coventry,* with her Sea Wolf missile system. Known as the 'Sea Dart-Sea Wolf combo' or the 'Type 42/22 missile trap', the tactic was intended to combine the benefits of both ships' radars and weapons, while at the same time multiplying the effectiveness of the Sea Harriers.

An engagement on the morning of May 24 seemed to suggest the tactic would work when HMS *Coventry* directed two Sea Harriers

Argentine Operational Air Order of Battle May 21, 1982

Laydown of main combat types committed to offensive operations

Naval Air Station Almirante Zar, Trelew, Chubut Province

8 x Canberra B.Mk62 (2nd Air Brigade)

Air Force Base Comodoro Rivadavia, Chubut Province

3 x Mirage IIIEA (8th Air Brigade)

Airfield Puerto San Julián, Santa Cruz Province

8 x IAI Dagger (6th Air Brigade)
10 x A-4C Skyhawk (4th Air Brigade)
4 x- Learjet 35A (Grupo Aérofotográfico, 1st Air Brigade)
2 x KC-130H Hercules Tanker (1st Air Brigade)
7 x Lockheed C-130E/H Hercules (1st Air Brigade)
3 x Boeing 707-320C (1st Air Brigade) (some early missions from Ezeiza International Airport, Buenos Aires)

Air Force Base Rio Gallegos, Santa Cruz Province

7 x Mirage IIIEA (8th Air Brigade)
15 x A-4B Skyhawk (5th Air Brigade)

Naval Air Station Almirante Quijada, Río Grande, Tierra del Fuego

10 x IAI Dagger (6th Air Brigade)
8 x A-4Q Skyhawk (3rd Naval Air Fighter/Attack Squadron)
4 x Super Étendard (2nd Naval Air Fighter/Attack Squadron)
2 x SP-2H Neptune (Naval Air Exploration Squadron)
5 x Grumman S-2E Tracker (Naval Air Antisubmarine Squadron)

to intercept three Daggers approaching at low level around the north coast of West Falkland. The Harriers downed all three jets before they could reach their targets.

The Battle of San Carlos had been won by the British. More than 4,000 British soldiers and Royal Marines had been put ashore safely on the Falklands. However, two warships had been lost and several other ships damaged. The Argentine air force and navy had lost 16 of its fast jets in their doomed effort to defeat the landing.

The Type 21 frigate HMS *Ardent* went down fighting while serving on the gun line after being hit by multiple bombs on May 21. *(DPL)*

HMS *Coventry* explodes after being hit by three Argentine bombs. *(DPL)*

MAY 25, 1982

The Sinking of the Atlantic Conveyor *and HMS* Coventry

Four days after the British landing at San Carlos, Argentine air commanders had adjusted their tactics in a bid to try to prevent more troops and supplies coming ashore. An improvised surveillance network involving Learjets, and C-130 Hercules transport aircraft was trying to pinpoint the location of British ships. Aircraft tracking radar at Port Stanley airport was also providing warning of the presence of British Sea Harrier patrols. Similarly, Argentine radar operators were able to work out the position of two Royal Navy carriers by tracking the Sea Harriers as they returned to their ships following patrols.

With the San Carlos anchorage now heavily defended, Argentine attention shifted to the British warships manning the missile trap position north of Pebble Island. A flight of four Skyhawks made a rare night-time approach to the Falklands in a bid to launch a surprise dawn attack, but one was detected by HMS *Coventry* at long range and shot down with a Sea Dart missile.

Later in the afternoon six Skyhawks were launched to attack the two British warships. Four jets made it to the target area and conducted a simultaneous attack from two separate directions, which confused the British defenders. A combination of misfortunes now unfolded. Sea Harriers were in position to intercept but were called off by HMS *Coventry*, which believed it could engage them with its Sea Dart. Then the Sea Dart system malfunctioned at a crucial moment, allowing the Skyhawks to close in the ships. HMS *Broadsword* tried to engage with its Sea Wolf, but it also failed to work. The first two Skyhawks dropped four bombs on the frigate. Three missed

The Type 45 destroyer, HMS *Coventry* capsized and sank within 20 minutes of the devastating attack. *(DPL)*

and one bounced over her flight deck, taking the nose off the ship's Lynx helicopter.

Within minutes the remaining two Skyhawks appeared and were heading for HMS *Coventry*. HMS *Broadsword* had now got its Sea Wolf system working and was locked-on to engage the attacking jets when HMS *Coventry* suddenly changed course to bring its Sea Dart to bear, but the manoeuvre masked the frigate's Sea Wolf. *Coventry* was now completely defenceless as the two jets overflew her and released their bombs. Three ripped into the side of her hull and exploded in the ship's computer room killing 19 sailors instantly. Her commanding officer, Captain David Hart-Dyke, was blown off his feet and recovered to find his operations room on fire. Within minutes the ship started to list and slipped under the waves. Miraculously 260 sailors survived and were rescued from the water.

The Argentine navy was not done. At Rio Grande airbase the Super Étendard squadron launched two of its jets to strike at the British carriers. During the evening of May 25, the Royal Navy planned to sail the large cargo ship *Atlantic Conveyor* into San Carlos Water to unload several helicopters and other stores. To give the ship as much time as possible to unload under darkness it had started to sail west during the afternoon with the naval task group, including the two carriers, to escort it.

This group of ships was detected by the Argentine jets just before dusk and two Exocets were launched at it. The in-bound missiles were detected by the frigates on the outer edge of the British task group which fired the chaff, immediately causing the missiles to swerve off and they tried to re-acquire new targets. The missiles found the 14,500 ton cargo ship and locked onto it. They slammed into the side of the ship and exploded. Fire engulfed the cargo deck and was rapidly approaching tanks of aviation fuel and cluster bombs when her master, Captain Ian North, ordered the crew to abandon ship. He was lost in the South Atlantic, along with 11 other crew. The ship initially stayed afloat, and a tug started to tow her, but the ship sank three days later. Six Wessex, three Chinook and one Lynx helicopter were lost in the fire on the ship, as well as equipment intended to set up a Harrier forward operating

The *Atlantic Conveyor* had already delivered vital additional Sea Harriers and Harrier GR3 jets to the task group before she headed to San Carlos Water to off load the remainder of her cargo, including Chinook and Wessex transport helicopters. *(DPL)*

site, tents, and signals intelligence equipment. This was a grave blow to the British campaign and meant the troops of 3 Commando Brigade would have to walk to Port Stanley.

The only positive news for the British was that the Argentine navy now only had one Exocet left. Although the Argentine pilots had inflicted heavy losses on the Royal Navy on May 25, this was very much the last throw of the dice for them. From now on the main action would take place ashore as British troops advanced on Port Stanley.

BAe Dynamics Sea Dart	
Weight	550kg (1,210lb)
Length	4.4m (14ft)
Diameter	0.42m (17in)
Warhead	11kg (24lb) HE blast-fragmentation
Wingspan	0.9m (3.0ft)
Operational range	74km (46 miles)
Flight ceiling	18,300m (60,000ft)
Maximum speed	Mach 3.0+

Salvage teams attempted to board the burnt out *Atlantic Conveyor*, but the ship and her cargo could not be saved. *(DPL)*

Captain Ian North, known affectionately across the task group as Captain Birds Eye after the character in the popular fish finger television advert, was lost minutes after he jumped into the sea from the *Atlantic Conveyor*. *(DPL)*

British Paratroopers round up prisoners during the advance towards the main Argentine defence line on the morning of May 28. *(DPL)*

VICTORY AT GOOSE GREEN

The First Land Battle of the War

As Argentine fighter jets battled with the Royal Navy warships around San Carlos Water, on shore the commander of 3 Commando Brigade, Brigadier Julian Thompson was preparing his troops to advance to Port Stanley. Every day ashore, they had more supplies and ammunition as a shuttle of ships arrived every night to unload their cargoes.

After only a few hours ashore, Thompson and his staff realised that the terrain of the Falklands was some of the most demanding they had ever faced. There were no roads, hardly any urban areas, high mountain ridges and huge peat bogs. It rained almost all the time.

Advancing across this terrain would only be possible with extensive helicopter support to move Thompson's artillery regiment and its ammunition, as well as food and water to keep his 5,000 troops fighting. Helicopters were the only way to rapidly evacuate wounded personnel back to the field hospital at Ajax Bay. Yet on May 25 Thompson had only 11 Sea King and Wessex helicopters available to support 3 Brigade. He was reluctant to advance without the means to keep

his troops supplied. When the *Atlantic Conveyor* was hit, taking her vital Wessex and Chinook helicopters to the bottom of the South Atlantic, Thompson's caution was reinforced. Better to wait for 5 Infantry Brigade and its additional helicopters before considering advancing.

That was not how it was seen in London. GCHQ eavesdroppers were decoding despondent messages from the Argentine headquarters in Port Stanley despairing at their lack of supplies, shortages of ammunition and the failure of the air force to stop the British landing. Thompson was summoned to the only satellite radio on the Falklands and instructed by the task group headquarters at Northwood to begin advancing, starting with a major raid against the Argentine garrison at Goose Green. The 2nd Battalion, The Parachute Regiment, or 2 PARA, under the command of Lieutenant Colonel H Jones was to march south from Sussex Mountain above San Carlos Water and attack the Argentine garrison. British intelligence estimated that there were only three or four enemy infantry companies at Goose Green, or between 400 and

Lieutenant Colonel H Jones led the 2nd Battalion, The Parachute Regiment, during the first hours of the Battle of Goose Green until he was killed in action. *(DPL)*

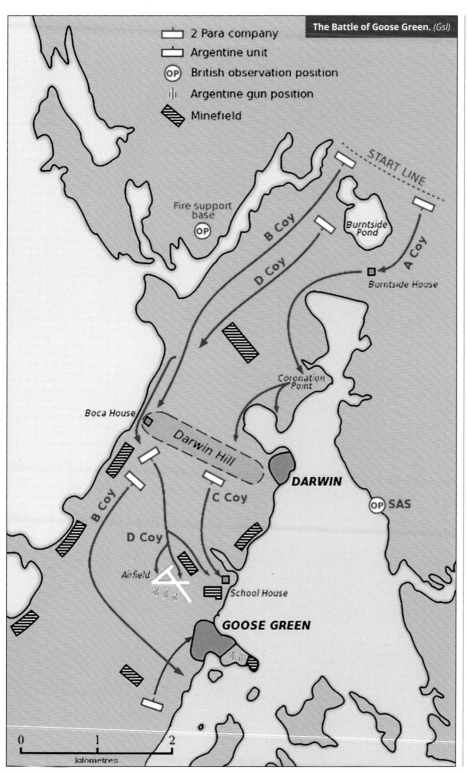

The Battle of Goose Green. *(Gsl)*

Legend:
- 2 Para company
- Argentine unit
- (OP) British observation position
- Argentine gun position
- Minefield

START LINE

Fire support base (OP)

B Coy

D Coy

A Coy

Burntside Pond

Burntside House

Coronation Point

Boca House

Darwin Hill

DARWIN

(OP) SAS

B Coy

C Coy

D Coy

Airfield

School House

GOOSE GREEN

0 1 2
kilometres

Royal Artillery 105mm Light Guns that would be flown down to set up a fire base once the battle started. A Royal Navy frigate was also to be on hand to provide naval gunfire support and RAF Harrier GR3 strike jets were also available. The RAF variant of the jump jet had just arrived on HMS *Hermes* after sailing south on the *Atlantic Conveyor*. Their pilots were specially trained in ground attack tactics. The loss of a Harrier GR3 to anti-aircraft fire over Goose Green on May 27 was not a good start to the operation.

During the daytime on May 27, advance 2 PARA patrols reached the vicinity of Goose Green and the nearby settlement of Darwin and traded fire with the Argentine defenders. Jones now issued his orders for the attack, which was to kick off in the early hours of the May 28. As 2 PARA was marching south the BBC World Service broadcast a report that the attack was underway after being briefed by 10 Downing Street. The British government wanted the public and the world to know 3 Commando Brigade was attacking. Jones and his troops were not impressed that the Argentines now knew what they were doing.

The Argentine 12th Infantry Regiment was dug in to protect the grass airstrip at Goose Green, which was home to several IA58 Pucara light strike aircraft. They had built a trench line across the isthmus to the north of the airstrip and built platoon-sized strongpoints on high ground at either end of the defensive line. The most experienced officers and soldiers in the garrison were posted to hold the strong points, which were able to sweep the isthmus with fire and prevent any movement towards the airstrip. As well as the 500 infantrymen of the 12th Regiment, there were more than 1,000 additional personnel, including artillerymen, air defence gunners and air force maintenance personnel. Many of the Argentine soldiers were conscripts who had only been in the army for three or four months.

One company of Argentine troops was posted forward of the main defence line as a tripwire to slow the British advance. Two companies of 2 PARA advanced in extended line down the isthmus and stumbled into the first line of Argentine troops in the dark. The British Paras found many of the Argentine conscripts hiding in the bottom of their foxholes. The remainder withdrew rapidly. The British continued to advance until they hit the main defence line as dawn was breaking.

With little cover, 2 PARA was forced to go to ground and trade fire with the Argentine strongpoints. The advance had been halted. There were mounting casualties on both sides. The Royal Navy frigate had run out of ammunition and the 105mm Light Guns were at the edge of

500 troops. Jones was confident his men's fighting spirit and tactical skill would make up for their lack of numerical superiority. Once they had captured the settlement, 2 PARA were to pull back to the main British perimeter. The raid was designed to give the Argentine army a bloody nose and boost morale back home.

The 600 men of 2 PARA headed south on the evening of May 26. They only had what supplies and ammunition they could carry on their backs for the 20 kilometre tactical advance to battle, or Tab to use airborne force's jargon. The only fire support for the raid was to be provided by three

There was no cover to protect the British Paratroopers during their advance on Goose Green. *(DPL)*

Only once the British Paratroopers has broken through the main Argentine defensive position could they advance on Goose Green itself. *(DPL)*

The place where Lieutenant Colonel H Jones fell was marked by a modest memorial. *(DPL)*

survivors of the western Argentine strongpoint surrendered. On the other end of the defence line, the defenders were systematically killed by the Paratroopers as they stormed each trench.

In the early afternoon, as the British were advancing again on the airstrip four Argentine aircraft made an attack run on the British position. Two Pucara and an Aermacchi MB33A were shot down by machine gunners and Blowpipe missiles before they could inflict any damage.

The last line of the Argentine defence were the anti-aircraft guns surrounding the airstrip which were now deployed in the direct-fire role against the British. Two RAF Harriers arrived to drop a string of cluster bombs across the anti-aircraft gun position. Then another Harrier strafed the final Argentine artillery position with cannon fire.

The Argentine position was now precarious despite the arrival of 150 reinforcements from Port Stanley by helicopter. Keeble entered into

their range so could not provide offensive fire support. This meant 2 PARA was on its own.

Colonel Jones moved forward to join the lead infantry companies to find out what was holding up the advance. He got within sight of the strongpoint on the eastern edge of the Argentine defence line and quickly realised that it would have to be cleared if the advance were to continue. He mustered a small group of Paratroopers and led them forward to assault the strongpoint. During this action he was shot and killed. He was the highest ranking British fatality of the conflict and would be posthumously awarded the Victoria Cross for his gallantry.

It now fell to the second-in-command of 2 PARA, Major Chris Keeble, to take over and lead the assault. The reserve company was brought up. Wire-guided anti-tank missiles and 66mm rockets systematically directed at the Argentine bunkers to silence their machine guns. A large group of Paratroopers crawled along the shore at the western edge of defence line to outflank the position. With fire falling from two directions and their retreat cut off, the

Stocks of Argentine napalm bombs had to be made safe by RAF bomb disposal officers after Goose Green fell. *(DPL)*

The remains of Argentine Pucara strike aircraft littered Goose Green airstrip. *(DPL)*

negotiations with the Argentine commander, Lieutenant Colonel Italo Piaggi, via a released prisoner of war and told them that unless the Argentine force surrendered a renewed assault would be launched in the morning. A ceasefire was agreed in the early hours of May 29 and the two officers met on the airstrip. The Argentine commander then agreed to surrender his troops. When they all paraded

on the airstrip to hand over their arms the British were staggered there so many of them.

The Battle for Goose Green was the bloodiest set-piece battle of the war, with 55 Argentine soldiers and 18 British personnel killed. More than 80 Argentines and 54 British were wounded. More than 100 Falkland Islanders who had taken shelter inside Goose Green settlement were freed.

Brigadier Thompson flew down to inspect the battlefield and congratulate 2 PARA on their victory. When he saw the volume of equipment that had been captured and the dejected nature of the Argentine prisoners, Thompson rescinded his orders for 2 PARA to pull back to San Carlos. The British were staying in Goose Green to provide a jumping-off point for their advance on Port Stanley.

The fallen of 2nd Battalion, The Parachute Regiment were buried in a field cemetery at Ajax Bay on May 30. *(DPL)*

ON TO MOUNT KENT

The British Advance on Port Stanley Begins

T he approach to Port Stanley is dominated by Mount Kent, the highest peak on East Falkland. Whoever controls Mount Kent can observe all below them. Brigadier Julian Thompson, the commander of 3 Commando Brigade, realised the importance of controlling the summit and was determined to move his artillery onto it to begin firing at Port Stanley. The lack of helicopters meant there was little chance of making a mass air assault onto the peak.

The Special Air Service (SAS) had maintained observation posts around Mount Kent since the start of the month to watch an Argentine helicopter base, and a rapid reaction infantry company on the western slope of the peak. The British soldiers had called in RAF Harrier GR3 strike jets to bomb the helicopters on two occasions since the landing at San Carlos, destroying several of them.

Thompson hatched a plan to fly the SAS's D Squadron on to Mount Kent to secure a landing zone for 42 Commando and three 105mm Light

After capturing Mount Kent, the SAS and Royal Marines had a commanding view of Port Stanley. *(DPL)*

The sole RAF Chinook, callsign Bravo November, played a critical role lifting 105mm Light Guns to the summit of Mount Kent. *(DPL)*

Royal Marines of 42 Commando took over Mount Kent from the SAS and secured it as a fire base for Royal Artillery 105mm Light Guns firing on Port Stanley. *(DPL)*

Guns to reinforce them. The first D Squadron contingent flew up to Mount Kent on May 24, but bad weather meant the following waves of reinforcements were stuck in San Carlos. The Argentine infantry company and the helicopters left on May 25 to reinforce the Goose Green garrison and were not replaced.

The commander of the SAS, Lieutenant Colonel Mike Rose saw this as a great opportunity to allow the British to seize unopposed the most important piece of terrain in the Falklands. More SAS men were flown up to the peak on May 28/29 and they reported back to Rose that the peak was secure. However, the SAS men were now coming under artillery fire and needed reinforcement quickly. The following night 100 Royal Marines loaded onto Sea Kings to fly up the mountain, but they had to turn back when the helicopters were engulfed in a white-out snow storm.

Colonel Rose organised another lift on the night of May 30/31 and this time the sole surviving RAF Chinook heavy lift helicopter would be pressed into service. The charismatic SAS officer called the Chinook pilots to a briefing.

It was an eye opener for one of them, Flight Lieutenant Andy Lawless, who had never worked with the SAS before. "Rose started asking if we could drop bombs off the rear ramp of the Chinook," recalled Lawless. "'Yes, or no?' he asked. The briefing quickly moved from the ridiculous to the sensible."

"We knew the SAS were outgunned," said Lawless. "Our job was to land 105mm [howitzers] of 29 Regiment. Rose told me the landing site was flat and secure. The mission was to be flown all at night with night vision goggles. We had three 105mm guns inside and ammunition pallets underslung."

Royal Marines from 42 Commando, including their commanding officer, Lieutenant Colonel Nick Vaux, arrived first to secure the peak. His troops spread around the peak in the midst of a snow storm.

Then the Chinook, using the iconic call sign Bravo November, arrived to drop off the first guns of 7 Battery of 29 Regiment Royal Artillery. "Once we dropped off the guns, we went straight back to San Carlos to bring in more guns and ammo," said Lawless.

If that was not eventful enough, Lawless and his pilot, Wing Commander Dick Langworthy, soon found themselves flying into a snow storm and then their night vision goggles began to fail. They flew into a lake and their cockpit was part submerged before the helicopter began to rise out of the water.

Back on Mount Kent, Rose had flown in on the first wave of helicopters and was soon overseeing a brief skirmish between his SAS men and an Argentine special forces patrol.

Vaux and Rose had a great view of Port Stanley below and on the morning of May 31, they ordered 7 Battery to fire several rounds at the old Royal Marines barracks at Moody Brook, to the west of the capital. In a typical Rose move, he had brought along the journalist Max Hastings, and he allowed him to use the SAS satellite radio network to file his copy back to Britain. The world now knew that the British were preparing to attack Port Stanley.

Teal Inlet on the north coast of East Falkland was a focal point for 3 Commando Brigade's build up of stores and ammunition stockpiles for the advance on Port Stanley. *(Lyubomir Ivanov)*

YOMPING
TO PORT STANLEY

3 Commando Brigade Marches to Battle

A t the same time that Brigadier Julian Thompson instructed Lieutenant Colonel H Jones and his paratroopers to attack Goose Green, the commander of 3 Commando Brigade issued orders to other units to advance along the northern coast of East Falkland.

With fewer than a dozen helicopters on hand, Thompson's troops would have to walk to Port Stanley. Leading the way on the northern axis were the Royal Marines of 45 Commando and close behind them came the 3rd Battalion, The Parachute Regiment (3 PARA).

There were no roads for the troops to march along – they had to navigate over peat bogs and hills to reach their objectives, often in pouring rain. There were not even any buildings or forests along their routes for the Royal Marines and Paratroopers to shelter in when they stopped to rest or cook ration packs.

To the Royal Marines this was 'Yomping'. The Paratroopers called it 'Tabbing' or a 'Tactical Advance to Battle'. The rivalry between Royal Marines and Paratroopers was legendary and they needed every ounce of high spirits to keep them going over the following week.

Royal Marines of 45 Commando led the march to Port Stanley along the northern route via Douglas Settlement and Teal Inlet. *(DPL)*

Royal Marines BV all-terrain vehicles and local tractors were the only vehicles that could move across country towards Port Stanley. *(DPL)*

On May 27, 45 Commando began their 20km Yomp to Douglas Settlement and 3 PARA set off later that day for Teal Inlet Settlement some 12km to the southeast. The Paratroopers picked a more direct route and were able to commandeer the services of several local tractors to help carry their mortars and ammunition. The Scimitar and Scorpion light tanks of the Blues and Royals were sent to help 3 PARA and they gave dozens of Paratroopers lifts as they sped across towards Teal Inlet.

By late on May 28 the two columns had reached their objectives after meeting no opposition. Thompson gave the exhausted troops a day to rest before he flew forward to give them new orders. Their new objective was Estancia House, just over 20km to the west of Port Stanley. This would bring 3 Commando Brigade within striking distance of the main Argentine garrison.

Thompson was now planning to airlift his small brigade headquarters to Teal Inlet when intelligence emerged that a team of Argentine special forces had landed by helicopter at Top Malo House on high ground overlooking the proposed new base for 3 Commando Brigade. An observation post of the elite Royal Marine Mountain and Arctic Warfare Cadre had spotted them. The Marine unit was ordered to mobilise its reserve personnel to neutralise the objective and on May 31 a Sea King helicopter flew the 19-strong assault team to a landing site near the farm buildings. In a matter of minutes, a fire support team had raked the wooden building with machine gun and 66mm rocket fire. The assault team then moved in to mop up as several of the Argentine troops

attempted to escape. Their leader was stopped in his tracks by two 40mm grenades. Five enemy soldiers were killed and 12 captured while three Royal Marines were wounded.

By June 1, 2 PARA had taken the high ground of Estancia House after another cross country Tab, but it was not until June 3 that it could be reinforced with 105mm Light Guns to give it the ability to target Argentine artillery in Port Stanley.

Teal Inlet was now secure, and Thompson's logistic problems were eased considerably on June 2 by the arrival of the landing ship, RFA *Sir Lancelot,* loaded with supplies. Soon Royal Artillery Rapier surface-to-air missile batteries were positioned around the

anchorage to defend the now regular shuttle of supply ships from being bombed.

Up on Mount Kent, the remainder of 42 Commando had taken up positions around the slopes of the peak. Then on June 4, 45 Commando moved to secure the high ground between Estancia House and Mount Kent to establish a solid front to the west of the main Argentine forces. It had taken just over a week for 3 Commando Brigade to march from San Carlos to the gates of Port Stanley. The move caught the Argentine command by surprise and even many British officers were amazed at the feat of endurance executed by 45 Commando and 3 PARA.

Royal Marines had to carry everything on their backs - food, ammunition, and water - during the Yomp to Port Stanley. *(DPL)*

CHINOOK
BRAVO NOVEMBER

British Helicopter Operations

On May 25, the *Atlantic Conveyor* was due to sail into San Carlos to off-load its precious cargo of helicopters and other supplies. Tragically, the Argentine pilots chose to launch an all-out attack on the British task group, firing two of their deadly Exocet sea skimming anti-ship missiles. Twelve men died and three RAF Chinook HC1 heavy lift helicopters of 18 (Bomber) Squadron were consumed in the fire, along with six Royal Navy Wessex HU5 and Lynx HAS3. By a stroke of luck, 18 (B) Squadron's other Chinook, code-named, Bravo November, was airborne on an engineering test during the Argentine missile attack and managed to make it to safety on board the carrier HMS *Hermes*.

A much reduced 18 (B) Squadron contingent then landed on the Falklands to prepare to operate Bravo November. Without tents, radios or any of the specialist tools and equipment needed to keep a Chinook flying, 18 (B) Squadron had to be taken in by 845 Naval Air Squadron at a forward operating location on the shores of San Carlos Water.

When 3 Commando Brigade went ashore on May 21 it only had 846 Naval Air Squadron, its Sea King HC4 and a handful of Wessex HU5s to move troops and supplies off the amphibious shipping. Keeping the Royal Artillery's Rapier air defence batteries re-supplied with fuel took up much of the helicopter force's time and fuel. There were just not enough helicopters available to move inland. The loss of *Atlantic Conveyor* and its three Chinooks

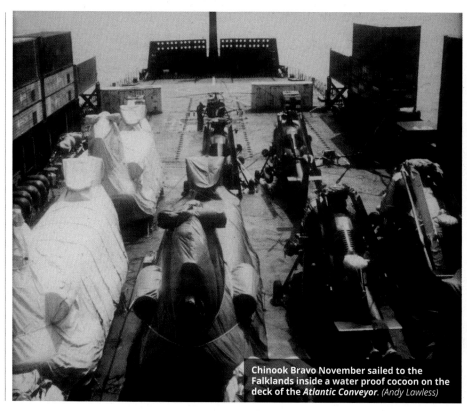

Chinook Bravo November sailed to the Falklands inside a water proof cocoon on the deck of the *Atlantic Conveyor*. *(Andy Lawless)*

made the situation even worse, prompting Brigadier Julian Thompson to comment, "we will have to walk then," when he heard the news.

Eventually the *Atlantic Causeway* and the helicopter support ship HMS *Engadine* arrived with more than three dozen helicopters, which allowed the offensive towards Port Stanley to get underway in earnest. By the start of June, the British had been able to mass around 50 Royal Navy transport helicopters, including Sea King HC4s, Wessex HU5s and stripped down anti-submarine HAS2s.

The Army Air Corps' 656 Squadron and 3 Commando Brigade Aviation Squadron RM were also ashore with their 15 Gazelle and 12 Scout utility helicopters, flying key commanders on visits to the front, evacuating causalities and occasionally engaging the Argentines with guided anti-tank missiles.

With no roads into the mountains, the only route to the front was by foot or helicopter. The Royal Marines and Paratroopers marched through the South Atlantic winter, but the vital guns of the Royal Artillery depended on Bravo November and smaller Royal Navy Wessex and Sea King helicopters to keep them firing.

Once fully operational, Chinook Bravo November did everything from moving troops to battle, flying ammunition to the front line, or lifting cargo off ships. *(DPL)*

After the surrender, Argentine POWs were pressed to work loading cargo onto Chinook Bravo November. *(Andy Lawless)*

Boeing Vertol Chinook HC1.	
Crew	3
Capacity	33–55 troops or 24 stretchers and 3 attendants
Sling-Load Capacity	26,000lb centre hook
Length	30m (98ft)
Fuselage length	16m (52ft)
Width	3.78m (12ft 5in)
Height	5.77m (18ft 11in)
Max take-off weight	22,680kg (50,000lb)
Maximum speed	315km/h (196mph)
Combat range	370km (200 miles)

Westland Sea King HC4	
Crew	2
Passengers	19
Length	16.69m (54ft 9in)
Length	22.15m (72ft 8in)
Height	4.72m (15ft 6in)
Max take-off weight	9,525kg (20,999lb)
Speed	209km/h (130mph)
Range	1,230km (664nm)
Armament	7.62mm GPMG door gun

After it arrived ashore, Bravo November was immediately used moving huge loads of ammunition from the British bridgehead to frontline artillery batteries. On one mission to fly 105mm Light Guns on to Mount Kent to support the SAS mission to capture the high ground, the Chinook crew's night vision goggles failed, and they flew into a lake. Bravo November held together and managed to get back to base. Its radio antenna had been ripped off, the autopilot had long failed, there were holes in the fuselage and a cockpit door was missing. The helicopter was gradually falling to bits and the lack of specialist lubricants meant its engine and gear box were always in danger of failing.

It did hold together for two more vital weeks as the British forces massed around Stanley for the finale of the war. During one flight, 81 Paratroopers were jammed into the back of the helicopter, almost double the normal load, for a dash to capture the settlement at Fitzroy. On its return journeys from the front, Bravo November brought scores of casualties back to the improvised field hospital at Ajax Bay.

By the time the Argentines surrendered, Bravo November had notched up 109 flying hours, carrying some 1,500 troops, 95 casualties, 550 POWs and 550 tons of cargo.

The Royal Navy, Royal Air Force and Army Air Corps helicopters had provided vital mobility and logistic support to the British ground forces. Without the artillery, ammunition and other supplies flown over the mountains to the front line near Port Stanley the British final push into the capital of the Falklands would not have been possible. Hundreds of wounded British and Argentine soldiers would have died where they fell if the British helicopters had not been able to rapidly lift them to medical help.

Gazelle helicopters of the 3 Commando Brigade Air Squadron were the jack of all trades, flying commanders on reconnaissance missions, evacuating casualties or delivering high value cargo to remote locations. *(MOD, via David Oliver)*

The trusty Wessex may have been on the verge of retirement from the support helicopter role by the Royal Navy before the Falklands War, but it proved to be a work horse during the campaign. *(US Navy)*

The bombing of the RAF *Sir Galahad* proved to be the greatest loss of British life in a single incident during the Falklands War. *(DPL)*

DISASTER AT BLUFF COVE

The Attack on RFA Sir Galahad

The television images of helicopters hovering near the burning landing ship RFA *Sir Galahad* to winch aboard survivors are some of the most powerful from the Falklands War. The ship and its sister, RFA *Sir Tristram,* had been hit by bombs dropped by Argentine Skyhawks in broad daylight. Fifty British soldiers and sailors were killed and 57 seriously injured. It was the largest loss of British life in a single incident in the war. Controversy continues to surround why so many troops were aboard the undefended ships. The roots of disaster stretched back to the arrival of the British 5 Infantry Brigade in San Carlos Water a week before on May 30.

Up to then all the British land forces had been commanded by Brigadier Julian Thompson of 3 Commando Brigade. On May 30, Major General Jeremy Moore came ashore at San Carlos to take over as Commander Land Forces Falkland Islands, or CLFFI. His two star, or divisional headquarters, would now control Thompson's brigade and 5 Brigade, which also started landing at San Carlos.

Thompson's brigade was already advancing around the northern route to Port Stanley and other Royal Marine units were on Mount Kent in the centre of East Falkland. The job of advancing along the southern route to

Gurkha troops assigned to 5 Infantry Brigade dig-in at San Carlos after landing at the beginning of June. They then moved to Goose Green to allow 2nd Battalion, The Parachute Regiment to move forward to Fitzroy. *(DPL)*

Troops of 5 Infantry Brigade started to come ashore at San Carlos from May 30. *(DPL)*

The logistics of moving 5 Infantry Brigade around from San Carlos to Fitzroy proved more difficult than expected. *(DPL)*

Port Stanley was given to the newly arrived 5 Brigade under its commander, Brigadier Tony Wilson. It was given command of the 2nd Battalion, The Parachute Regiment (2 PARA) at Goose Green, but otherwise all its troops, equipment and supplies were at San Carlos.

Somehow, they all had to be moved to the gates of Port Stanley, nearly 100km away. The Welsh Guards attempted to march to Goose Green to join 2 PARA, but they were not as fit as the Paratroopers or Royal Marines and had to turn back. A new plan was needed.

Down at Goose Green, Tony Wilson was trying to come up with ideas to get his advance moving when troops from 2 PARA found that there was a telephone line from a remote settlement called Swan Inlet to Fitzroy some 40km east of Goose Green. Securing Fitzroy would bring 5 Brigade within striking distance of the southern defences of Port Stanley. On June 2, a raiding party of Paratroopers flew in three Scout utility helicopters to Swan Inlet and made the call to Fitzroy. Locals told them that the Argentines had left, and the settlement was undefended.

Wilson now ordered the Scout helicopters to move another reconnaissance team of Paratroopers to land at Fitzroy. Once they confirmed that the settlement was indeed empty, Wilson effectively hijacked the only RAF

Once she had been hit, the RAF *Sir Galahad* was ablaze in a matter of minutes trapping scores of soldiers from the Welsh Guards on board. *(DPL)*

Chinook, which had just landed at Goose Green to begin transporting Argentine prisoners of war to San Carlos. The Brigadier pulled rank and within minutes 80 Paratroopers were crammed inside Chinook Bravo November for the hop to Fitzroy. They nearly didn't survive after Royal Marine observers on Mount Kent spotted the unauthorised helicopter mission. Thinking it was an Argentine Chinook, the Marines ordered an artillery fire mission on the landing zone, which was only called off at the last minute when the RAF markings were spotted on the side of Bravo November. Fitzroy was now secure and 5 Brigade had its forward operating base.

General Moore, Brigadier Wilson and the commander of the amphibious task group, Commodore Mike Clapp, now wanted to use the assault ships HMS *Fearless* and HMS *Intrepid* to sail 5 Brigade from San Carlos and put them ashore at Fitzroy. The commander of the naval task group, Rear Admiral Sandy Woodward vetoed the plan as too risky. The Argentine army still controlled the high ground overlooking Fitzroy and any ship in the vicinity would be a sitting duck for shore-based Exocet missiles based near Port Stanley. A compromise was agreed. Each of the assault ships would make the journey around the south of East Falkland carrying one of 5 Brigade's infantry battalions and then launch their landing craft out at sea to carry the troops to Fitzroy to keep the assault ships out of range of the Exocets. The first mission by HMS *Intrepid* on June 5 successfully landed the Scots Guards but it took seven hours for the landing craft to reach shore in heavy seas. On the next night HMS *Fearless* tried to repeat the exercise carrying the Welsh Guards. The landing craft that had carried the Scots Guards ashore had been supposed to come out from Fitzroy to collect the new unit. They were not ready after their mission the night before so only half of the Welsh Guards could be put ashore in HMS *Fearless'* two landing craft. The remainder of the battalion were returned to San Carlos and Commodore Clapp's staff produced a new plan to get them to Fitzroy.

They were loaded onto the RFA *Sir Galahad* which was heading to Fitzroy overnight on June 7/8. Admiral Woodward reluctantly agreed to the plan because he believed the ship could get into Fitzroy and quickly off-load the troops before the Argentines realised what was happening. There

An improvised rescue effort brought the survivors of the attack ashore. *(MOD)*

had been bad weather over the past couple of days which added to feeling it was a risk worth taking. Events conspired to end in disaster.

June 8 turned out to be a brilliantly clear day. The rapid re-jigging of the plan the day before meant that the *Sir Galahad* was also carrying Rapier missiles and a field ambulance unit. They were destined to go ashore at Bluff Cove just down the coast from Fitzroy. The commanders at Bluff Cove were not told the ship was coming so did not muster their landing craft in time to take off all the troops in one go. The Rapiers had to be lifted off by helicopter and then the field ambulance needed to be off-loaded so the Welsh Guards had to wait inside the ship. It was a 20 mile march to Fitzroy and their officers wanted to wait until the ship could sail to their intended destination. A Royal Marine officer tried to persuade them to disembark but the Guards officers stuck to their orders.

When the *Sir Galahad* arrived, its sister ship was still at anchor. It had been the intention that only one landing ship at a time would be in Bluff Cove to avoid attracting attention, but her ramp had been damaged so her unloading had been delayed.

As feared by Admiral Woodward, Argentine observation posts had spotted the ships and an air strike was ordered. Five Skyhawks reached the target area after a Sea Harrier combat air patrol had been diverted to deal with another air raid. Even though the Rapiers had been landed from *Sir Galahad* the missiles were still being set up when the air raid began. The Argentine jets arrived over Bluff Cove late the afternoon and immediately launched their attack.

As they made the attack run, the jets opened fire with their cannons punching holes in the sides of the ships. Two bombs hit RFA *Sir Tristram*. One blew off her ramp and the other failed to explode. Two crew were killed by cannon fire, but the ship was empty, and the crew were able to abandon ship with no more loss of life.

A landing craft from HMS *Fearless* was also sunk on June 8 by a follow-up wave of Argentine A-4 Skyhawks. *(Naval History)*

The Welsh Guards on board *Sir Galahad* were less fortunate. More than 200 soldiers were crammed on her vehicle deck when three bombs punched through the hull. A subsequent Admiralty board of inquiry concluded that the bombs did not explode but the penetrating weapons started fires as they ripped apart the ship. The cannon fire from the Skyhawks added to the inferno and soon fuel for the generators from the Rapier battery caught fire. Within minutes the troop deck was engulfed in a fireball. Hundreds of Welsh Guards were trapped on the burning deck.

Much of the ship's superstructure was made of aluminium and started to melt. Quick thinking Royal Marines from the ship's boat party started to evacuate casualties out of the bow ramp into small boats and life

rafts. Soon dozens of men were in the water. An emergency call was put out and every available helicopter in the area started to converge to rescue the survivors. Eventually more than 150 traumatised survivors were airlifted to the field hospital at Ajax Bay. RFA *Sir Tristram* was eventually salvaged but the smouldering hulk of the RFA *Sir Galahad* was eventually towed out to sea and sent to the bottom as a war grave.

Although the loss of life was horrendous and the graphic television images of the wounded being brought ashore caused consternation back in Britain when broadcast, the loss of the two ships in the end had little impact on General Moore's campaign. Most of 5 Brigade and its supplies had been delivered to Fitzroy. The two Welsh Guards companies were replaced by troops from 40 Commando. In the end the final attack on Port Stanley was only delayed by two days.

The Admiralty board of inquiry was finally released in 2007 and it chose not to apportion blame for the two ships being attacked, saying no individual action led to the heavy loss of life. It concluded that the commanders who sent RFA *Sir Galahad* into harm's way were trying to speed up the end of the war. It was a calculated risk that didn't pay off.

Soldiers of the Scots Guards at Bluff Cove engaged the attacking Argentine aircraft with their GPMGs but to little effect. *(DPL)*

RFA *Sir Galahad*	
Round Table class LSL	
Builder	Alexander Stephen and Sons, Glasgow
Laid down	February 1965
Launched	April 19, 1966
Displacement	5,765 tons fully loaded
Length	126m (412ft)
Beam	18m (60ft)
Speed	31km/h (17kts)
Complement	68 crew, up to 534 passengers
Armament	Two 40 mm Bofors AA guns

GENERAL MOORE'S BATTLE PLAN

The British Close on Port Stanley

During the first days of June, Major General Jeremy Moore was cajoling his two brigade commanders to get their troops into position to attack Port Stanley. The winter weather was approaching, and the commander of British land forces knew he had to defeat the Argentinians quickly or risk the war sinking into a long, drawn-out stalemate. The increasingly stormy weather was battering the Royal Navy warships of the task group. The clock was ticking.

The bulk of the Argentine ground forces – more than 5,000 out of 11,000 personnel left on the Falklands - were deployed around Port Stanley, occupying a series of hilltop strongpoints or coastal defence positions. These troops had spent more than six weeks fortifying their positions, digging trenches, and building bunkers, as well as laying thousands of land mines. From their hilltop positions, the Argentine troops had good fields of fire to take on any assault force.

To capture these positions, General Moore was going to rely on artillery to force the enemy to take cover and give his troops the chance to advance in safety. The 105mm Light guns of two Royal Artillery field regiments - 29

Commando Regiment and 4 Regiment - were flown forward to provide this fire support.

The British attack was to take place at night, to give the advancing troops the advantage of surprise. General Moore was convinced his Royal Marines, Paratroopers, Guardsmen and Gurkhas were better trained at night fighting than their opponents. He was also confident they could find their way through the Argentine minefields undetected and then press home their attack in darkness. Once on top of the enemy trenches, the British troops would clear the Argentine trenches and bunkers with bayonets and grenades.

By the end of the first week of June, the two British brigades were within striking distance of Port Stanley, but General Moore had not yet decided on the final details of his attack. The crucial limiting factor was getting enough ammunition to the gun positions and infantry battalions. There were no roads up to the forward positions in the hills around Port Stanley – all the 105mm shells, 81mm mortar rounds, and boxes of small arms ammunition had to be airlifted by helicopters. Originally, Moore's planner had projected that 1,000 shells per 105mm Light Gun would be needed to fight the battle. The General said they would

Providing enough shells and bullets to frontline troops was essential to the success of Major General Jeremy Moore's battle plan to take Port Stanley. *(DPL)*

There were just not enough helicopters to go around so the fighting troops had to march to Port Stanley. The helicopters carried the ammunition and other supplies. *(DPL)*

Troops of the Commando Logistic Regiment worked around the clock to unload supplies and ammunition from ships and landing craft. *(DPL)*

have to make do with half that number. Every helicopter was pressed to carry ammunition forward. Casualty evacuation helicopters were even loaded with ammunition when they flew up into the mountains to collected wounded soldiers. Senior officers had to sit on boxes of small ammunition and grenades when they flew up to the forward units in the Gazelle and Scout utility helicopters.

Moore was still working out the best direction to break into the Argentine defensive position. The Royal Marines, under Brigadier Julian Thompson, were pressing for 3 Commando Brigade to lead the way from the west. Brigadier Tony Wilson's 5 Infantry Brigade wanted to strike north from their forward base at Fitzroy. The two brigade commanders lobbied for their ideas and demanded priority for helicopter support to bring forward the supplies they both needed.

On June 9, Moore went firm on his plan. He decided to let 3 Brigade take the lead in a systematic operation to roll up the Argentine defences from the west. Thompson's 42 and 45 Commando, as well as 3rd Battalion, The Parachute Regiment would take Mount Harriet, Two Sisters and Mount Longdon respectively. Then on the following night, 5 Brigade would swing into action to capture Mount Tumbledown and Wireless Ridge. A final push would then take place to clear the last defences before Stanley.

The Royal Marines and Paratroopers of 3 Brigade were told to be ready to attack during the night of June 11/12. This would give them time for final reconnaissance patrols and rehearsals before they crossed their start lines.

Argentine Military Garrison – Port Stanley Region
Commander: Brigade General Mario Menéndez

10th Mechanised Infantry Brigade
Land Forces Commander: Brigadier-General Oscar Luis Jofre
3rd Infantry Regiment
6th Infantry Regiment
7th Infantry Regiment
25th Infantry Regiment

Artillery
3rd Artillery Group
18 OTO Melara Mod 56 105mm field guns
2 x CITER 155mm L33 Guns
4th Airborne Artillery Group
18 x 10mm guns.

Miscellaneous Army Units
181st Military Police and Intelligence Company
601st Engineer Company
9th Engineer Company
10th Engineer Company
601 Commando Company
602 Commando Company
601 Combat Aviation Battalion

'Reserva Z'
Panhard Armoured Car Squadron (12 x Panhard Armoured Cars)
10th Armoured Cavalry Reconnaissance Squadron (dismounted)
6th Regiment's 'Piribebuy' Company
3rd Regiment's 'Tacuari' Company

Marines
5th Marine Infantry Battalion.
1st Marine Field Artillery Battalion's B Battery

Gendarmería Nacional (Border Guards)
601 Special Forces Company

Major General Jeremy Moore after helicoptering on board HMS *Hermes* to meet task group commander, Rear Admiral Sandy Woodward. *(MOD)*

BOMBARDING
PORT STANLEY

Softening up the Argentine Defences

To give the assault troops the best chance of success, the Royal Navy and Royal Air Force ramped up their bombardment of the Argentine garrison in Port Stanley. They wanted to stop any more reinforcements being flown in to the beleaguered garrison and further undermine their morale by making sure they got as little sleep as possible. A rolling programme of bombardments accelerated during the first days of June.

Each night Royal Navy frigates and destroyers were dispatched to form a gun line off Port Stanley to bombard the Argentine positions with their 4.5-inch guns. The warships also had the advantage of carrying their own ammunition which reduced the need to fly ammunition up to Royal Artillery gun batteries.

The weight of fire put down by the ships was massive with the five main warships involved firing more than 5,000 4.5-inch shells during the bombardment effort. HMS *Glamorgan* fired 1,245 shells, HMS *Avenger* 1,075, HMS *Yarmouth* 1,441, HMS *Arrow* 905 and HMS *Active* 633.

The airfield to the east of the island's capital was a priority target and Argentine fuel and ammunition dumps came under regular attack. Other naval gunfire support was targeted at the

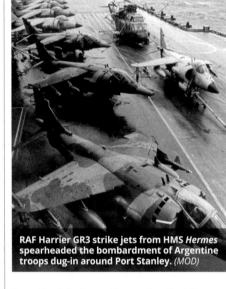

RAF Harrier GR3 strike jets from HMS *Hermes* spearheaded the bombardment of Argentine troops dug-in around Port Stanley. *(MOD)*

AGM-45 Strike anti-radiation missiles were fired from RAF Vulcan bombers in a bid to close down the Argentine radars at Port Stanley. *(MOD, via David Oliver)*

Argentine infantry positions out on the hills to make sure the dispirited conscripts manning them got no sleep. British artillery observers made a point of targeting any enemy troops moving in the open to stop supplies being moved up to front line positions. These attacks had the desired effect. By the time the British attacked, the Argentine conscripts were reduced to eating cold rations or killing sheep to survive.

The RAF GR3 ground attack Harriers were now flying daily missions against Port Stanley, both

Long range Argentine radars at Port Stanley airport tracked British aircraft and ships operating around the Falklands. *(Think Defence)*

A truck mounted Exocet missile launcher was flown out to Port Stanley in a bid to drive off British warships bombarding the airport. *(Think Defence)*

from HMS *Hermes* and a forward airstrip built by the Royal Engineers near San Carlos Settlement. They dropped a mix of 1,000lb iron bombs, BL755 cluster bombs and Paveway laser guided bombs on troop positions and Port Stanley airfield.

In response to the intensifying British naval bombardment, the Argentine navy had stripped an Exocet missile launcher from one of its corvettes and flown it to the Falklands in the back of a C-130 Hercules. This wheeled launcher was first fired unsuccessfully at a British warship in May, and it was subsequently hidden whenever British aircraft appeared overhead. To destroy the Westinghouse AN/TPS-43 long-range 3D radar that the Argentines were using to give warning of British air raids, the RAF mobilised its Vulcan bombers again. This time they were fitted with US-supplied AGM-45 Shrike anti-radiation missiles, which were designed to home in on enemy radar emissions.

Three *Black Buck* missions were planned against the Argentine radar. One was cancelled during an air-to-air refuelling problem on May 28, but missiles were fired on missions

on May 31 and June 3. On its way back to Ascension Island the final Vulcan had another air-to-air refuelling problem and had to divert to Brazil, where it was detained for several days. The troublesome Argentine radar remained in service until the end of the war.

For the opening British land attack on Port Stanley on June 11, the Royal Navy ordered four warships - HMS *Glamorgan*, HMS *Avenger*, HMS *Yarmouth* and HMS *Arrow* - to close with the islands and to support the advancing troops.

During the all out effort, the Argentine Exocet team made one final foray out of their hide to engage the British warships. They had been ordered to remain just outside of the enemy missile's range, but *Glamorgan* came too close to shore. The missile crew were waiting and fired off one missile that hit the destroyer's helicopter hangar, killing 13 sailors. They were the last Royal Navy personnel to die in the conflict. The destroyer was so badly damaged it took no further part in the war.

Despite the heavy casualties on HMS *Glamorgan* more ships - HMS *Avenger*, HMS *Yarmouth*,

HMS *Active*, and HMS *Ambuscade* - were dispatched to join the gun line for the final attack on Port Stanley on the night of June 13-14. This was not considered the time to lift the pressure on the defenders of Port Stanley.

Hawker Siddeley Harrier GR3	
Crew	1
Length	14.27m (46ft 10in)
Wingspan	7.75m (25ft 5in)
Max take-off weight	11,431kg (5,200lb)
Maximum speed	1,176km/h (731mph)
Combat range	670km (410 miles)

Armament

Guns – 2 × 30 mm ADEN cannon pods under the fuselage

Rockets – 4 × Matra rocket pods with 18 × SNEB 68mm rockets each

Missiles – 2 × AIM-9 Sidewinder air-to-air missiles

Bombs – A variety of unguided iron bombs, BL755 cluster bombs or laser-guided bombs

A land-based French-made Exocet anti-ship missile. *(Aerospatiale/MBDA)*

Paratroopers wait to move forward in the build up to the assault of Mount Longdon. *(DPL)*

MOUNT LONGDON

3 PARA's Toughest Battle

The first British unit to attack was the 3rd Battalion, The Parachute Regiment (3 PARA) under the command of Lieutenant Colonel Hugh Pike. The unit's objective was Mount Longdon, which was defended by the Argentine 7th Infantry Regiment.

Mount Longdon is a ridge feature running west to east toward Port Stanley with a kilometre-long narrow summit. The defenders were dug-in along the ridge, which gave them commanding views of the approaches to their positions.

Colonel Pike's troops had been probing the ground for several days gathering intelligence to allow him to work out how to attack the strongpoint. His plan involved multiple phases, with a four hour march under the cover of darkness to the battalion's start line around a kilometre from the objective.

The battalion was ordered to begin its attack at a minute past 8pm but its assault companies got delayed by 15 minutes trying to navigate the boggy terrain.

A Company was to clear the northern slope of Mount Longdon and B Company was to sweep east along the southern slope. The rest of the battalion, including its mortars, Milan anti-tank missiles and GPMG heavy machine guns, would remain on the start line to provide fire support.

The open terrain around Mount Longdon provided little shelter from Argentine observation or artillery fire. *(DPL)*

At first the approach went well with the Argentines unaware what was happening after they switched off their ground surveillance radar to prevent it being detected. The defenders thought the British would attack at dawn not in the middle of the night.

The element of surprise was lost when a B Company soldier stood on a mine and was seriously injured. B Company now rushed forward to begin clearing the Argentine trenches. British and Argentine troops were now fighting at point blank range, one trench or bunker at a time.

Argentine troops were positioned along the length of Mount Longdon with overlapping fields of fire making it difficult for B Company's attack to gain any momentum. Its centre platoon was soon pinned down and its commander seriously wounded. Sergeant Ian McKay took over command and tried to get his men moving forward. More were killed and wounded by a dug-in heavy machine gun. He led an attack on the position but was killed a few minutes later. After the battle, his body was found inside the enemy sangar. For his bravery, Sergeant McKay was posthumously awarded the Victoria Cross, the second for the Parachute Regiment in the war.

The enemy proved to be too well dug in for the remnants of B Company to deal with, so its commander decided to make a tactical withdrawal to allow the Argentines to be pounded with artillery, mortars, and naval gunfire. Colonel Pike was now up with B Company and re-cast his plan.

A Company had been pinned down by artillery and heavy machine gun fire after crossing the start line. Pike ordered them to pull back and swing back into dead ground on the western slope of Mount Longdon. They then moved south and came up behind B Company, ready to fight through to clear the eastern edge of the summit. The extra troops and additional fire support proved too much for the Argentines, who were now pulling back from their positions. As dawn was breaking, 3 PARA was in control of Mount Longdon.

The battle saw the bloodiest land fighting during the final push for Port Stanley, with 17 Paratroopers killed and more than 40 wounded.

Wounded Paratroopers are evacuated from Mount Longdon on the morning after their successful attack to capture the mountain feature. *(DPL)*

Soldiers from 3rd Battalion, The Parachute Regiment, celebrate after the ceasefire is called on June 14. *(DPL)*

Royal Artillery 105mm Light Guns provided covering fire throughout the attack on Mount Longdon. *(DPL)*

At least 29 Argentine soldiers were killed during the fighting and around 50 were captured. The rest pulled back to Wireless Ridge to the east. For 3 PARA the fighting was not over. As soon as the Argentines were off the hill, their artillery started to shell their old positions with considerable accuracy, forcing the British soldiers to take shelter in the abandoned bunkers and trenches. Over the next 48 hours a further six members of 3 PARA were killed by artillery and mortar fire.

L7 General Purpose Machine Gun	
Weight	11.8kg (26.01lb)
Length	1,263mm (49.7in)
Cartridge	7.62×51mm NATO
Action	Gas-operated long-stroke piston, open bolt
Rate of fire	650–1,000 rounds/min
Effective firing range	800m (875 yards) (bipod); 1,800m (1,969 yards) (tripod)

Royal Marines of 45 Commando on Two Sisters. *(DPL)*

TWO SISTERS

45 Commando Goes on the Attack

T o the south of Mount Longdon was another ridge line, dubbed Two Sisters, so-called because it comprised two summits made up of large rock slabs. The easterly summit was codenamed Summer Days by 45 Commando who were tasked with capturing the position. The westerly summit was codenamed Long Toenail by the Royal Marines.

Lieutenant Colonel Andrew Whitehead devised a daring plan to capture Two Sisters in a two pronged attack. His X Company would advance from a westerly direction to seize the Long Toenail and then set up a fire base to support Y and Z Companies as they assaulted the remainder of the feature from the northwest.

Defending Two Sisters was a scratch force made up of two companies drawn from the Argentine's 4th and 6th Infantry Regiments, with a combined strength of around 300 troops. They had only been moved into position a few days after the San Carlos landings in May as the threat of a British attack from the west emerged. As a result, there

A helicopter re-supply of 81mm mortar rounds to 45 Commando in the build-up to the attack on Two Sisters. *(DPL)*

Once Two Sisters was captured, 45 Commando had to search and secure more than 50 Argentine prisoners. *(DPL)*

The two pronged attack on Two Sisters broke the Argentine defences. *(Naval History)*

was not a co-ordinated defence of the feature, with each company reporting to a different regimental headquarters. The troops did not have time to prepare their positions or plant heavy minefields.

The plan called for X Company, reinforced with Milan anti-tank missiles from 40 Commando and 84mm Carl Gustav recoilless rifles, to be in position by 8.30pm but the heavily laden troops took twice as long as expected to reach their start line. They were not in position until 11pm. In the meantime, the rest of 45 Commando was approaching its start line.

Colonel Whitehead now decided to accelerate the advance of Y and Z Companies and not wait for X Company to provide fire support. Just as the companies were forming up to attack, Argentine artillery fire started to land in front of Z Company. The troops held their positions to wait until the fire lifted.

X Company was now in position and started its attack. The Royal Marines moved forward and found the lower slopes of Long Toenail mostly undefended. They had almost reached the feature's summit when X Company came under fire from three machine gun posts. Milan missiles were brought to bear and then Royal Marines started to assault the remaining enemy trenches.

Y and Z Companies had kept up their advance and got to within a few hundred metres of the summit of Summer Days without the Argentines spotting them. The lead Royal Marines then spotted Argentine troops using their night sights, so they went to ground to allow their commanders to work out how to attack. A flare was fired over the Royal Marines by the defenders, prompting the outbreak of a firefight. The British called down artillery fire on the enemy positions.

Rather than get pinned down in the open, the commander of Z Company decided to push on. To cries of the company battle cry, "Zulu, Zulu", the Royal Marines charged the Argentine positions as artillery, mortars, GPMGs, 84mm Carl Gustavs, and 66mm anti-tank rockets rained down on the ridge

line. Y Company now started to switch its fire to support the advance by Z Company to its left.

Z Company's advance swept up to the summit of Summer Days and by 2.45am they had driven the last of the Argentine defenders away. Y Company was now able to advance to clear the western edge of the feature and by dawn X Company had cleared its objective.

The battle for Two Sisters had cost 45 Commando four dead and 10 wounded. Ten Argentines were killed and 54 captured, with the rest making their escape into the night. All the British losses had been to artillery and mortar fire rather than small arms during close quarter fighting.

Despite having good fields of view over the approaches to their positions, the Argentines hoped that their artillery, mortars, and heavy machine guns would keep the British at bay. When the Royal Marines kept moving in spite of being under heavy fire the defenders decided to fall back rather than go toe to toe with their opponents.

When Colonel Whitehead reported in to Brigadier Julian Thompson that he had captured all his objectives for minimal losses, he requested permission to keep advancing to exploit his success. The commander of 3 Commando Brigade told him to hold his position. The Battle for Port Stanley was far from won.

Casualties were evacuated from the battlefield by Scout helicopters. *(DPL)*

HARRIET

MOUNT HARRIET

42 Commando's Outflanking Move

The final unit of 3 Commando Brigade to go into battle on the night of June 11/12 was 42 Commando under the command of Lieutenant Colonel Nick Vaux. Their objective was a large feature known as Mount Harriet. There was a secondary ridge line a few hundred metres to the north known as Goat Ridge. The area was defended by more than 400 troops of the Argentine 4th Infantry Regiment, who had spent several weeks building bunkers and laying minefields. The Argentine commander positioned most of his troops on the western slopes of Mount Harriet and Goat Ridge, where he expected the British attack to come.

Colonel Vaux was determined not to attack the Argentines head on, and he had spent several days conducting a detailed reconnaissance of the enemy positions. Night patrols had probed the edges of the Argentine position and two of his Royal Marines lost feet to land mines during these missions. Covert observation posts of the Mountain and Arctic Warfare Cadre had been set up to watch the Argentine positions and spot any weaknesses in their defences.

His patrols had worked out that by swinging to the south of Mount Harriet by two kilometres his troops would skirt past the main Argentine positions and minefields. So, Vaux decided to adopt a very different approach to 3 Brigade's other units. Two companies of 42 Commando would take the longer route and then form up to the southeast of Mount Harriet and attack it from behind. As this manoeuvre was underway, Vaux's J Company would stage a feint attack from the west to convince the Argentines that the main attack was coming from this direction. It was intended that K and L Companies would be in position to start their outflanking attack at 9pm. However, the whole attack was delayed by nearly an hour after J Company and the reconnaissance platoon of the Welsh Guards, who were to support them, could not find each other in the dark.

Columns of Royal Marines march off Mount Harriet with a group of Argentine prisoners. *(DPL)*

During their long approach march, the Royal Marines had to dive for cover when illuminating mortar rounds were fired above them, but they were not spotted and arrived at their start line just before 10pm. J Company was now ready and began their noisy distraction operation.

Once the advance to contact was ordered, the Royal Marines of K Company covered more than 700 metres before they were noticed. The British troops were in the process of moving through the tented camp of the Argentine mortar platoon at the rear of Mount Harriet when a single shot broke the silence. Close quarter fighting erupted as the Royal Marines cleared out the sleeping Argentine troops.

Several Argentine machine guns and snipers now engaged K Company high up on the ridge line. The Royal Marines began to systematically clear these positions, with fire support teams with GMPGs and 66mm rockets putting down suppressive fire to allow assault teams to crawl forward to post grenades or shoot the defenders.

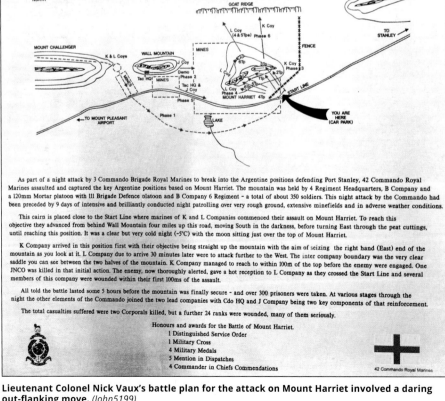
Lieutenant Colonel Nick Vaux's battle plan for the attack on Mount Harriet involved a daring out-flanking move. *(John5199)*

L1A1 Self Loading Rifle (SLR)	
Royal Small Arms Factory	
Weight	4.337kg (9.56lb)
Length	1,143mm (45in)
Cartridge	7.62 × 51mm NATO
Action	Gas-operated, tilting breechblock
Rate of fire	Semi-automatic
Effective firing range	800m (875 yards)

A Sea King delivers supplies to 42 Commando in the run up to the Battle of Mount Harriet. *(DPL)*

The whole exercise was over very quickly as the highly trained Royal Marines dispatched the disorganised defenders.

Now L Company joined their action, but they were spotted earlier and had to spend five hours clearing the objectives after bringing up Milan missiles to engage the Argentine machine gun positions. The Royal Marine unit staged several section assaults on enemy positions to move forward until they were on the summit of Mount Harriet. British troops overran the 4th Regiment's headquarters, sending senior officers fleeing into the darkness. In the final minutes of the battle a lone Argentine sniper held out at the top of the ridgeline. He injured several Royal Marines until an 84mm Carl Gustav was brought up to silence him.

By dawn, Vaux and his men were in full control of Mount Harriet. Their surprise attack meant they trapped the bulk of the 4th Regiment and the Royal Marines spent most of the morning of June 12 rounding up nearly 300 prisoners. Around 10 Argentines were killed. No organised groups of Argentines managed to get off the mountain. Only one Royal Marine was killed and 10 more wounded.

Lieutenant Colonel Nick Vaux relaxes with some of his Royal Marines after the battle. *(DPL)*

The view from Mount Tumbledown looking down on Goat Ridge, where the Scots Guards formed up for their attack. *(Scots Guards)*

MOUNT
TUMBLEDOWN

The Scots Guards Strike

On the morning of June 12, as the advance units of 3 Commando Brigade settled into their newly occupied positions it was the turn of 5 Infantry Brigade to strike. The original plan was for Brigadier Tony Wilson's units to attack during the following night, but he wanted to give his troops more time to prepare.

Major General Jeremy Moore and Brigadier Wilson held a council of war during the morning of June 12 at Brigadier Julian Thompson's headquarters. 5 Brigade would now attack on the evening of June 13. Its assault units would be brought up in helicopters from their positions around Fitzroy into assembly areas to the west of the high ground recently captured by 3 Brigade.

5 Brigade's attack would be spearheaded by the 1st Battalion, The Scots Guards, under the command of Lieutenant Colonel Mike Scott. Their objective was Mount Tumbledown to the east of Mount Harriet. It was defended by a company of around 150 Argentine Marines,

The Scots Guards were flown by helicopters from Fitzroy to a forming up point to the west of Mount Tumbledown. *(Navy Wings)*

which comprised well armed and well trained professional soldiers and long service conscripts.

Colonel Scott planned to clear Mount Tumbledown by sweeping along the ridge from west to east. He intended to attack one company at a time to seize a third of the mountain at a time, leap frogging new companies through the recently captured positions.

To give his assault troops a chance to get close to the Argentine positions, the Scots Guards reconnaissance platoon was sent on a diversionary mission to the south of Mount Tumbledown to distract the defenders' attention. Four of the Blues and Royals Scimitar light tanks were attached to make the enemy think this was the main direction of attack.

This attack kicked off at 8.30pm and had the desired effect but the diversion force got stuck in a minefield and then attracted mortar fire. Two soldiers were killed and four wounded, but the incident drew heavy fire from several Argentine positions.

As this was underway, the lead Scots Guards crossed their start line west of Tumbledown at 9pm and advanced swiftly up the western slope of the feature without being detected. G Company went firm on its objectives, and it was now time for the Left Flank Company to move through to assault the central section of the ridge. They were soon engaged by Argentine Marine snipers with night-sight equipped weapons. Mortar and artillery fire was brought down on the Scottish soldiers and several Guardsmen were killed and wounded.

The top of the ridge was covered in large rocky crags that made perfect defensive positions. They had wide fields of fire and overhead protection to make it difficult to neutralise them with artillery or mortar fire.

The only way to advance was for the Guardsmen to crawl forward and post grenades in enemy positions before assaulting them with fixed bayonets. The company

Scots Guards celebrate capturing the summit of Mount Tumbledown. *(MOD)*

commander led the assault, shooting two Argentines dead and bayoneting a third. Once his troops had reached their objective, the company commander found himself on top of Mount Tumbledown with just seven uninjured soldiers.

Colonel Scott now moved the Right Flank Company up onto Mount Tumbledown to continue the advance. They also met skilful resistance from the Argentine Marines, and it took them until well after dawn to clear out the last enemy position with bayonets and grenades.

The battle cost the Scots Guards five dead and two more were killed in mortar fire as the regiment assumed positions to defend the mountain. More than 40 Scots Guards were wounded. The Argentine defenders suffered

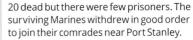

A Royal Marines Gazelle evacuates a casualty from Mount Tumbledown on the morning after the battle. *(MOD, via David Oliver)*

20 dead but there were few prisoners. The surviving Marines withdrew in good order to join their comrades near Port Stanley.

Once the Scots Guards had secured Tumbledown, Brigadier Wilson ordered the 1st Battalion, 7th Duke of Edinburgh's Own Gurkha Rifles (1/7 GR) to move forward to seize Mount William. They skirted around the north of Mount Tumbledown and then passed through the centre of the Scots Guards to form up to assault their objective. Before the famous Nepalese soldiers could get into action, the Argentine Marines on Mount William rapidly withdrew. The Gurkhas occupied the feature unopposed.

After the battle Argentine prisoners were rounded up by the Scots Guards. *(DPL)*

Royal Ordnance 105mm Light Gun	
Weight	1,858kg (4,096lb)
Length	8.8m (28ft 10in)
Width	1.78m (5ft 10in)
Crew	6
Rate of fire	6–8 rounds per minute
Maximum firing range	17,200m (18,800 yards)

WIRELESS RIDGE

2 PARA Overwhelms the Last Argentine Defence Line

As the Scots Guards were busy fighting their way along Mount Tumbledown the second deliberate assault of the night June 13/14 was unfolding a few kilometres to the north.

The operation to capture Wireless Ridge, to the west of Mount Longdon, would clear up 3 Commando Brigade's northern flank and give Brigadier Julian Thompson's troops a direct route to push into the open ground around Port Stanley.

This mission would fall to the 2nd Battalion, The Parachute Regiment (2 PARA), who had switched back to 3 Brigade on June 11 to act as a reserve force when Thompson's men launched their main attack. They had been harboured up around Mount Estancia waiting for the order to be called forward but 3 Brigade did not need their help. In the wake of 3 Brigade's success, 2 PARA was now warned off for the Wireless Ridge operation.

2 PARA had a new commanding officer, Lieutenant Colonel David Chaundler, who had flown out from Britain to take over the battalion in the wake of H Jones' death at Goose Green the previous month. Chaundler parachuted into the South Atlantic from a Royal Air Force C-130 Hercules before being picked out of the icy water and taken aboard a Royal Navy frigate. His men were relieved to be placed back under 3 Brigade

A Paratrooper stands ready with his GPMG to see off any Argentine counter-attacks on Wireless Ridge. *(DPL)*

Lavish fire support from almost every weapon in the British arsenal, including 105mm Light Guns, was laid on to support the assault on Wireless Ridge. *(DPL)*

Army Air Corps Scout helicopters flew up to Wireless Ridge to recover wounded Paratroopers. *(DPL)*

and excited at getting a chance to lead the next phase of the assault that could end the war.

Their objective was held by the two companies from the Argentine 7th Infantry Regiment and some stragglers from the unit who had survived the assault on Mount Longdon. In total there were probably no more than 300 under-equipped, poorly armed, and demoralised conscripts defending the low-lying ridge feature. It comprised two summits in the centre of the feature and another smaller summit to the south, just in front of the old Royal Marines barracks at Moody Brook.

Brigadier Thompson provided 2 PARA with lavish fire support for the assault, including 105mm Light Guns, naval gun fire, mortar, Milan anti-tank missiles, and heavy machine gun support. Harrier GR3 attack jets also pounded Argentine positions around Moody Brook earlier in the evening with Paveway laser guided bombs. Mobile fire support was on hand from four Scimitar light tanks of the Blues and Royals, which were assigned to advance alongside the Paratroopers.

The operation kicked off just after 9pm on June 13 with a complex fire plan that involved almost every weapon assigned to the support of 2 PARA. This was unlike anything that had been seen before in the campaign. The barrage lasted a few minutes and then D Company started to move forward against the western summit.

Argentine troops could be seen standing up and fleeing their trenches. When D Company reached the summit, they found the position all but abandoned. Thirty seven Argentine conscripts were captured cowering in their trenches. The Scimitars now raced up the ridge to join the Paratroopers as they

After securing Wireless Ridge, the main job of the British Paratroopers was to round up Argentine prisoners. *(DPL)*

provided fire support for B Company as it assaulted the eastern summit. Once again, the Argentine troops fled rather than stand fighting. They retreated so rapidly that the Paratroopers found abandoned radios and field telephones that were still working and linked to the 7th Regiment's headquarters.

The finale of the battle was D Company's assault on the southern summit. This was the last hill feature before Moody Brook, so the Argentine troops were determined to make a fight of it. Despite an intensive barrage, D Company had to put in a deliberate assault and start to clear the Argentine trenches. At this point the enemy troops realised the game was up and fled rather than get into close quarter fighting.

While the Argentine infantry did not put up much of a fight on Wireless Ridge, their artillery was quick to bring down fire on the Paratroopers. For nine hours they shelled the feature causing one death among the British. Another was killed in a firefight and a third fatality was killed by an errant British shell. Eleven Paratroopers were wounded. Fifteen Argentine soldiers from the 7th Regiment were killed and dozens injured in the battle.

The Argentine command now realised the danger the British attack posed and mobilised its last reserves to counter-attack. The 70 crewmen from the reserve armoured car squadrons were mobilised into an infantry force and a company from the 3rd Infantry Regiment was loaded on trucks in Port Stanley and driven out toward Moody Brook.

Just after dawn the counter-attack force formed up in extended line and began to advance on Wireless Ridge. Up on the high ground, 3 PARA opened up with every weapon they had. Three of the attackers were killed and dozens injured. The rest dived for cover and then retreated back to Port Stanley. It was described by some participants as a turkey shoot.

Within hours of taking Wireless Ridge the 2nd Battalion, The Parachute Regiment was marching into Port Stanley. *(DPL)*

Royal Marines of 45 Commando march into Port Stanley with flags flying. *(DPL)*

THE ARGENTINE RETREAT

The Final Day of Fighting

As dawn was breaking on June 14, British troops had broken the resistance of the last Argentine positions outside Port Stanley. British commanders on the hills around the town were watching disorganised groups of Argentine troops moving west into the islands' capital. There seemed to be little organised resistance beyond an artillery battery west of Moody Brook, which was still firing on Wireless Ridge and a company of Argentine Marines on Sapper Hill, directly to the south of Port Stanley.

Three British Scout utility helicopters of 3 Commando Brigade Air Squadron were rapidly armed with SS-11 wire guided anti-tank missiles and sent up to engage the gun battery. They were poised to fire their weapons when Argentine anti-aircraft guns opened up, forcing the helicopters to retreat to a safer distance. Brigadier Julian Thompson ordered 3 Commando Brigade to begin a general advance to the western edge of Port Stanley town to keep the Argentines on the run.

5 Infantry Brigade now ordered up the Welsh Guards to mount a rapid assault on Sapper Hill to prevent the Argentines forming a final defensive line on the low lying feature. Two companies of Royal Marines of 40 Commando assigned to the Welsh Guards were loaded in Sea Kings to fly them forward to an assembly area. However, three of the helicopters landed the Marines too close to the enemy and a firefight ensued. Two Marines were wounded, and three Argentines were killed. The British were pinned down for much of the morning as they re-organised themselves. An artillery fire barrage was requested to

Gurkhas captured Mount William after the Argentine defenders fled. *(DPL)*

The Blues and Royals drove their armoured vehicles into Port Stanley. *(DPL)*

Columns of Royal Marines were inside Port Stanley soon after the surrender document was signed. *(DPL)*

suppress the defenders to allow the Royal Marines to mount a ground assault. A flight of RAF Harrier GR3s armed with cluster bombs was lined up to bomb the hill, to open the attack. With only minutes to spare the attack was called off when news started to emerge that the Argentines might be surrendering. This chaotic action proved to be the last fighting of the battle for Port Stanley.

Inside Port Stanley, the Argentine command was in crisis. Brigade General Mario Menéndez had several radio conversations with the head of the Junta in Buenos Aires, General Leopoldo Galtieri. He could not believe the situation was so bad and ordered Menéndez to counter-attack

with his three infantry regiments based around the airport. The Falklands commander told his president that the battle was lost.

Late on June 13, the ground forces commander, Brigade General Oscar Jofre, told Menéndez he could perhaps organise a retreat to the airport and make a last stand there. But the rapid advances by the British to Moody Brook and the developing attack on Sapper Hill meant there was little chance of setting up a last line of defence to cover the withdrawal. Menéndez realised the game was up. He made one last radio call to Galtieri at 10am and told the head of the Junta to open negotiations with the British to accept the United Nations

Security Council resolution that called on the Argentine garrison on the Falklands to return to the mainland. Galtieri would have none of it. Menéndez told his President that he would take responsibility for what happened on las Malvinas. He had resolved to surrender to stop any more of his troops being slaughtered.

In one of the great ironies of history, Menéndez did not realise how precarious a position the British were in. The 105mm Light Guns were down to less than eight rounds each. Troops out on the hills were exhausted after three days of non-stop action and it had started to snow. The Argentine will to fight expired just before the British means to fight was exhausted.

A strike by RAF Harrier GR3s on Sapper Hill was called off at the last minute. Here laser guided bombs are being loaded on a RAF jet on HMS *Hermes*. *(MOD, via David Oliver)*

Port Stanley was surrendered without a fight by the Argentines on the afternoon of June 14. *(DPL)*

WHITE FLAGS
OVER STANLEY

The Surrender is Signed

Lieutenant Colonel Mike Rose's troops did not have a big role in the final battle for Port Stanley. His Special Air Service (SAS) troopers had done their job providing vital intelligence for the Royal Marines, Paratroopers and Guardsmen to launch their attacks on the main Argentine positions. They now had to sit back and watch the action. There was one last hurrah during the battle for Wireless Ridge when an SAS raiding party in boats staged a diversion to distract the defender's attention from the Parachute Regiment's deliberate attack.

Colonel Rose had been making himself useful in other ways. For several days he had been waging a psychological warfare campaign against the Argentine garrison. GCHQ signals intelligence had alerted the British to the increasingly despondent tone of Brigade General Mario Menéndez's reports back to the Junta. So, Rose hoped to capitalise on this by using a network of civilian amateur radio operators to try to convince the Argentine general to surrender before it was too late. A Spanish-speaking Royal Marines officer, Captain Rob Bell, began to broadcast appeals over the radio network offering to open talks with Menéndez to end the fighting.

These broadcasts became known to one of Menéndez's staff officers, Captain Barry Melbourne-Hussey. The English-speaking officer told his general about the British offer after he had made his last call to the head of the

Junta in Buenos Aires on the morning of June 14. Menéndez ordered Melbourne-Hussey to arrange a meeting to discuss terms. This was accepted by Major General Jeremy Moore, the British land forces commander. Rose and Bell agreed to meet Menéndez in Port Stanley at 3pm. The agreement prompted Moore to order an end to all offensive operations and led to the attack on Sapper Hill being called off with minutes to spare at around 1pm. Moore ordered the British artillery to cease fire and for his troops to stop advancing when they reached the edge of Port Stanley. Amid the pause in the fighting, the British journalist Max Hastings decided to walk into the town and claim to the be the first member of the task force to enter free Port Stanley.

After flying to the meeting by helicopter, Rose quickly realised that all the fight had gone out of Menéndez who only seemed interested in retaining his military honour. He rapidly agreed to meet General Moore later that day to formally surrender. The Royal Marine General flew into Port Stanley just after 7pm to meet his opponent, who arrived in full dress uniform. The appearance of the Argentine general surprised Moore who thought he was facing a different General Menéndez. Moore had followed the tradition of the World War Two British General Bernard Montgomery and kept a photograph of his opponent in his cabin on the liner *Queen Elizabeth II* as he sailed south to the Falklands in the hope of gaining an

insight into his character. Rather than a fighting general who had led the Dirty War against insurgents, the officer in charge of the Falklands was an unassuming character who looked akin to a bank manager. British intelligence had mixed up its General Menéndezes.

Upstairs in the old British administration's secretariat building the two generals discussed the final terms. Moore played up that the Argentine soldiers had done their duty and there was nothing to be gained from further

Spanish speaking Royal Marine Captain Rob Bell played an instrumental part in negotiating the surrender of Argentine forces in Port Stanley. *(DPL)*

bloodshed. When Menéndez asked for the word 'unconditional' to be struck out of the surrender document, Moore readily agreed. He was not going risk the deal breaking down over a single word. Rose used the SAS satellite radio network to flash a message via the regiment's headquarters in Hereford to the task force headquarters in

Northwood confirming the surrender document had been signed. Minutes later the news was passed to the Prime Minister in Downing Street.

Outside, General Menéndez's troops were beating a hasty retreat to the airport and the first British units were moving into the town. Moore left the secretariat building

to walk around Port Stanley and talk to the newly liberated Islanders. He apologised for "taking three and half weeks to get here."

With darkness falling the rival armies tried to find some shelter from the freezing weather. Everyone was exhausted and just wanted to sleep.

> **A flash message confirming the surrender was sent to Task Force Headquarters at Northwood over the SAS satellite communications network.** *(Dick Brettbohrer)*

```
150120Z JUN 82

FM TPS HEREFORD
TO CTF 317
      CTG 317.8
      CTG 317,0
      CTG 317.9

INFO   CTU 317.1.1
       CTU 317.1.2

UNCLAS

SIC   19F

THE FOL IS THE TEXT OF A MSG FROM 317.1 PASSED VIA HEREFORD TO ADDRESSEES
ABOVE.  MSG BEGINS.
HQ LFFI PORT STANLEY.  IN PORT STANLEY AT 9 O'CLOCK PM FALKLAND ISLANDS
TIME TONIGHT THE 14 JUNE 1982, MAJOR GENERAL MENENDES SURRENDERED TO ME
ALL THE ARGENTINE ARMED FORCES IN EAST AND WEST FALKLAND, TOGETHER WITH
THEIR IMPEDIMENTA.  ARRANGEMENTS ARE IN HAND TO ASEMBLE THE MEN FOR RETURN
TO ARGENTINA, TO GATHER IN THEIR ARMS AND EQUIPMENT, AND TO MARK AND MAKE
SAFE THEIR MUNITIONS.  THE FALKLAND ISLANDS ARE ONCE MORE UNDER THE
GOVERNMENT DESIRED BY THEIR INHABITANTS.
GOD SAVE THE QUEEN.
SIGNED J J MOORE.
MSG ENDS
```

Major General Jeremy Moore greets Falkland Islanders in Port Stanley after the surrender. *(DPL)*

Scimitars of the Blues and Royals were quickly moved into Port Stanley to make clear to the Argentines who was in charge now. *(DPL)*

CLEARING UP
THE ISLANDS

Removing the Debris of War

On the morning of June 15, Major General Jeremy Moore's troops set about rounding up and disarming the 10,000 strong Argentine garrison in Port Stanley. These disorganised, demoralised, and starving soldiers had no will to fight any more and were only interested in going home.

British troops set up disarmament points to strip them of their arms and ammunition and then marched the prisoners off to the airport, which was rapidly being turned into a huge POW camp. There was only a narrow isthmus connecting the airport to Port Stanley town, so it was relatively easy to guard them. They had little inclination to escape in the freezing Falkland winter.

British merchant ships with contingents of soldiers on board were sent to the isolated settlements on West Falkland to collect the 1,000 or so Argentine troops defending them.

With no shelter to house the prisoners and even less food to feed them, General Moore decided that the best thing to do was ship them straight home to Argentina. The 1,500 troops captured at Goose Green in May had already been shipped home via Uruguay. Within a matter of days, the liner *Canberra,* loaded with more than 4,000 POWs, set sail for Argentina. The liner was directed to an isolated port in southern Argentina to off-load its cargo on June 20. More ships followed over the next few days. The Argentine military was desperate to keep the return of its soldiers on British ships from adding to its humiliation.

General Leopoldo Galtieri resigned on June 17 after rioting had broken out in Buenos Aires once news of the surrender had emerged. The military's control on the

Royal Marines began processing the thousands of Argentine prisoners on the morning of June 15. *(DPL)*

country was slipping and within months a civilian government would return to power.

The surrender signed by Brigade General Mario Menéndez only applied to the Argentine forces on the Falkland Islands rather than a formal ceasefire that covered all of the South Atlantic. In London, the British government was worried that the Argentine air and naval forces would wage a campaign of air and naval harassment of the Falklands. The government in Buenos Aires would not enter into talks with the British, beyond granting safe passage for

the POW repatriation ships. So, the British kept 500 senior officers back as bargaining chips to ensure good behaviour by Buenos Aires. This proved fruitless and by the end of July the remaining prisoners, including Menéndez, were sent home on the ferry *St Edmond.*

Around Port Stanley, the British garrison was busy trying to tidy up the town, collecting up all the abandoned Argentine weapons and marking the minefields that surrounded the area. British troops began to build a cemetery for the war dead at San Carlos

Royal Navy hospital ships soon began transporting wounded POWs back to Argentina. *(DPL)*

Thousands of unexploded bombs, shells and mines littered Port Stanley airport. *(DPL)*

and a major effort was made to gather up Argentine dead from their abandoned positions. Representatives of the International Committee for the Red Cross were eventually invited to the island to oversee the burial of the Argentine soldiers near Darwin.

A major effort was put into making the airfield operational again to allow Royal Air Force C-130 Hercules to land. The RAF Harrier GR3 Harriers also re-located from HMS *Hermes* and the San Carlos forward operating site to Port Stanley airport to provide limited air defence of the island's capital.

Ships of the Royal Navy task group started to make port visits so repairs could be made, and the sailors were given the chance to go ashore. The absence of a formal ceasefire meant the Royal Navy carriers and their Sea Harriers were still needed to provide strategic air defence of the Falklands.

The final chapter of the war took place on June 20 when the patrol ship HMS *Endurance*, escorted by the frigate HMS *Yarmouth*,

landed a party of Royal Marines on the island of South Thule. The remote island was part of the Cook Island territory. The Royal Marines met no resistance from the

11 Argentine naval personnel who had been in residence since 1976 operating a weather station. British control had been restored to its territories in the South Atlantic.

The RAF was quick to open Port Stanley airport to C-130 Hercules aircraft that flew from Ascension Island with the help of air-to-air refuelling. *(DPL)*

Over the summer of 1982, RAF Harriers moved into Port Stanley airport. *(MOD, via David Oliver)*

Royal Marines retook the island of South Thule, which had been occupied by Argentine Marines since 1976, on June 20, 1982. *(DPL)*

THE TASK FORCE
RETURNS

Britain Brings Home its Troops

Once the bulk of the Argentine POWs had been returned home, attention turned to reducing the number of British forces on the Falklands. The troops had won the war and now they were keen to get home to their families.

There was a need to maintain a garrison to deter future Argentine attacks on the islands. A follow-up wave of ships, troops and aircraft would soon be heading south to take over as the peacetime garrison of the Falklands. It would take time for these forces to get to the islands.

The first troops to head home where the Royal Marines and Paratroopers of 3 Commando Brigade. They sailed home in some style onboard the liner *Canberra*, which arrived to a massive welcome in Southampton on July 11. Ten days later the carrier HMS *Hermes* and the assault ships HMS *Fearless* and HMS *Intrepid* arrived home to Portsmouth to a similarly rapturous celebration.

5 Infantry Brigade remained in Port Stanley as the garrison and its troops would not be home until the end of the British summer, which of course, meant the Falklands' winter.

Other ships returned to their home ports over the summer, and it was not until HMS *Invincible* sailed into Portsmouth in September that the last major warships were home. She had been replaced by HMS *Illustrious* in August, after the new carrier had been rushed through a crash programme to complete her construction.

Royal Navy warships, including HMS *Invincible*, received joyous welcomes back to Portsmouth and other naval bases. *(MOD)*

Hundreds of military personnel were decorated for gallantry in the conflict. *(DPL)*

Tens of thousands of family members and well wishers turned out to greet the returning warships, army units and air force squadrons. *(DPL)*

The nuclear-powered submarine HMS *Conqueror* had a less high profile welcome when she slipped into Faslane on July 3. She was flying the Jolly Roger pirate flag to symbolise a successful operational patrol. The flag was emblazoned with a silhouette of the Argentine cruiser ARA *General Belgrano*. Within months the submarine's action would be the centre of a political storm.

Prime Minister Margaret Thatcher was keen to stage a welcome home for the task force. In October 1982, the Falkland Victory Parade was held in the City of London and some 300,000 people lined the streets to cheer on the troops.

An important symbolic event was the return of Governor Rex Hunt to Port Stanley. He arrived in his bi-corn hat and full colonial-era regalia.

An important milestone was achieved on June 24 when the first Royal Air Force Hercules landed after the crater in the runway caused by the first Black Buck Vulcan had been repaired. The runway was extended over the summer and eventually RAF F-4 Phantom fighter jets arrived to provide a permanent air defence capability. This finally allowed the RAF Harrier force to return home.

A strong RAF contingent remained on Ascension Island to run the air bridge to the Falklands. This journey still needed to be operated by Hercules aircraft that had to be refuelled in mid air. This was a long and uncomfortable journey for passengers in the cargo cabin of the airlifter.

The air bridge carried its most famous passenger in January 1983 when Margaret Thatcher flew down to visit the Falklands. Her Hercules was provided with a special comfort pod with airliner standard seats, bunks, and sound-proofing. She spent four days in the Falklands to a rapturous welcome from the Islanders. After visiting the battlefields, meeting troops, and sailing into San Carlos Water on a Royal Navy destroyer, the Prime Minister told islanders that "Britain planned to defend the islands for a very long time."

Britain had paid a high price for its victory, with 255 British military personnel killed and

777 wounded. By August 1982, the South Atlantic Fund had raised more than £11m from a generous public to help wounded veterans and to support the families of the war dead. The highest profile wounded

veteran, Welsh Guardsman Simon Weston, had been badly burnt during the attack on RFA *Sir Galahad*. Simon won universal praise for his dignified struggle to overcome his injuries and his work as a charity campaigner.

Prime Minister Margaret Thatcher made a triumphant visit to the Falkland Islands in January 1983. *(MOD)*

The Big While Whale, the liner *Canberra*, brought 3 Commando Brigade home. *(DPL)*

Air-to-air refuelling had to be used to keep the air bridge to Port Stanley from Ascension Island open. *(MOD, via Andy Thomas)*

Royal Navy air defence missiles, such as the Sea Dart, performed poorly in the Falklands war. *(MOD)*

LEARNING THE LESSONS

The Impact of the Falklands War

Forty years on from the Falklands War it is possible to reflect on what the conflict meant for Britain and Argentina and their respective armed forces, as well as the development of defence technology and the execution of military operations.

Victory in combat meant Britain's soldiers, sailors and airmen received a triumphant welcome from a grateful nation. The leaders of the military effort were promoted. Admiral Sir John Fieldhouse, the commander of the task force, rose to head the British armed forces and other senior officers assumed new and higher ranked positions. The Defence Secretary John Nott, who had proposed sweeping cuts to the Royal Navy in the run-up to the war, decided to retire from politics in 1983 and was replaced by the flamboyant Michael Heseltine.

Mrs Thatcher and her Conservative government rode a wave of popularity to win the 1983 general election with an enhanced majority. She remained in office until 1990.

This was in stark contrast to what happened on the Argentine side. The leaders of the military Junta were pushed from power days after the defeat and democracy restored. In 1983 the leader of the Junta, General Leopoldo Galtieri, was arrested on charges of human rights abuses during the so-called Dirty War of the 1970s, as well as for mishandling the Falklands War. The details of the bungling by the senior military leadership were fully revealed in the Rattenbach report in 1983. The report, created following Argentina's inquiry into the conflict praised the bravery of junior Argentine officers, pilots and soldiers and accused the senior officers of not using their forces properly or providing them with suitable equipment and training.

In Britain, the attitude of the government and senior military leaders to errors and technical problems was very different. Admiral Sir John Fieldhouse took the view that "washing its dirty laundry in public" would be bad for military morale. No officers were disciplined for the

The Sea Harrier jump jet was Britain's most successful killer of Argentine aircraft during the war. *(MOD, via David Oliver)*

A lack of airborne early warning bedevilled the British campaign and was only rectified by the rapid installation of a radar on Sea King helicopter. The first one arrived in the Falklands in the autumn of 1982 onboard HMS *Illustrious*. *(MOD)*

sinking of HMS *Sheffield* or the attack on RFA *Sir Galahad*, both of which led to considerable loss of life. The Admiralty board of inquiry reports were kept secret for more than 20 years.

This was a very different era. Britain's armed forces were held in very high esteem by both government and public. Today, after the lamentable performance of the 'Snatch' Land Rover, body armour, and RAF bombs in the Kosovo, Iraq and Afghan wars public perceptions, media coverage and the attitudes of politicians are very different. Back in the 1980s the war against the IRA was still going on in Northern Ireland and the Soviet Union was a clear and present danger, so maintaining the reputation of Britain's military commanders and the armed forces' equipment was considered vital. The influence of the defence industry was also brought to bear and details of the poor performance of British-made weapons, particularly the Blowpipe and Rapier air defence missiles, was kept secret to protect their export prospects. Details of the lobbying to keep embarrassing details out of the public domain was revealed by Professor Lawrence Freedman in his official history in 2006.

The Falklands War was the first naval conflict of the guided missile age, and the power of these weapons was brutally demonstrated by the devastation of HMS *Sheffield* by a French-made Exocet sea skimming missile. While the Argentines achieved an impressive hit rate with their Exocets - five air and one ground

launched, hitting three ships – the British air defence missiles proved less impressive. Analysis of British missile engagements from ships revealed that the fundamental problem was a lack of reliability that meant at critical moments, control switches did not work because of corrosion, software crashed, or missiles refused to fire. The land-based missiles suffered worse because of lack of spare parts and the impact of being stowed in the open during the voyage to the Falklands. During the Battle of San Carlos, the Royal Navy re-learnt the lesson that putting up a wall of machine gun and cannon fire can have a disproportionate impact on incoming strike jet pilots, forcing them to take evasive action and so miss their targets.

In the following decades, the Royal Navy sorted out many of the bugs in their missile systems, warships were fitted with Phalanx gun close-in weapon systems that can shoot down Exocet-type missiles and crucially an airborne early warning helicopter was rapidly brought into service to provide 'over the horizon' radar coverage for naval task groups. In the late 1990s, Royal Navy attack submarines were fitted with the long range Tomahawk land attack cruise missiles to allow them to strike at targets, such as airbases, deep behind enemy lines with pinpoint accuracy. In future Britain's Special Forces would no longer need to contemplate suicide missions to attempt to knock out enemy airfields housing guided missile armed jets threatening the Royal Navy.

In the months following the war the infamous cuts to the Royal Navy were reversed and almost all of the sunken warships and auxiliary ships were replaced as British defence spending spiked during the remainder of the decade. The fall of the Berlin Wall in November 1989 meant this would again be reversed as a series of governments started to claw back a peace dividend.

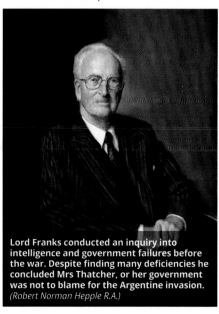

Lord Franks conducted an inquiry into intelligence and government failures before the war. Despite finding many deficiencies he concluded Mrs Thatcher, or her government was not to blame for the Argentine invasion. *(Robert Norman Hepple R.A.)*

Mount Pleasant Airbase is the hub of British military operations in the South Atlantic. *(MOD)*

FORTRESS FALKLANDS

The Islands and Britain's Garrison Today

After decades of saying it would not keep a significant military garrison on the Falklands to deter an Argentine attack, in the aftermath of the 1982 war the British government decided to do just that.

The crucial component in securing the island from future attacks would be the establishment of an airbase that could accommodate modern fast jet fighters to secure air supremacy over the South Atlantic. This airbase would also allow the rapid reinforcement of the islands by widebody transport aircraft in time of crisis.

So, in June 1983 the British government announced that work would begin on such a facility, near Mount Pleasant, 43 kilometres southwest of Port Stanley. This would allow the existing airport at Stanley to remain open during the three year long construction period. A new port also had to be built to allow the construction material and equipment to be landed for the £215m project.

Once it was declared fully operational in February 1986, RAF Mount Pleasant became the British military headquarters in the South Atlantic and the hub for the UK garrison.

Since then, the heart of the British garrison has been its four RAF fighter jets, which were based inside hardened aircraft shelters and stood ready on 24/7 quick reaction alert or QRA

duty. Initially these were US-made Phantom FGR2s until they were replaced by Tornado F3s in 1992. In 2009 the first Typhoon jets arrived at

RAF Mount Pleasant, and they remain on duty there today. While the Phantom and Tornado F3s were specialist air defence jets, the Typhoon

British soldiers have garrisoned the Falklands since 1982, although today less than 900 service personnel are routinely based on the islands. *(MOD)*

Argentine politicians continue to lay claim to 'Las Malvinas', but the country's military is now a shadow of its former self and lacks the capability to seize the islands. *(Casa Rosada Argentina)*

The British military garrison has brought stability and security to the islands. Its population has nearly doubled since 1982 to just under 4,000. Fishing has boomed and income from licences has meant the Falkland Islands government has been running a budget surplus for the past 30 years. Tourism is also a key part of the island's booming economy. Oil and gas exploration has not yet turned into production operations, but the climate change agenda means the islands could become a home for giant wind farms. As result, the islanders have one of the best standards of living in the world.

Argentina's return to democracy has meant the prospect of another war seems unlikely. The country's economic problems have also limited its funding for its armed forces, and they do not have the capability to take on the small British garrison on the Falklands, particularly the RAF Typhoons. Yet neither the Argentines nor the British have shifted from their rival territorial claims on the islands. Neither side has any interest or inclination to try to move the status quo.

is a true multi-role aircraft and can take on air, land, and naval threats with a variety of guided weapons. No air force in South America, including Argentina's, has anything to match the Typhoon and its suite of long-range stand-off missiles, making it unlikely that any invasion force would get anywhere close to the Falklands.

With air supremacy assured over the South Atlantic, and its reinforcement air route secured to the RAF-controlled airfield on Ascension Island, Britain has run down the land and sea-based elements of its Falklands garrison. It is currently home to just under 900 military personnel who live in the massive complex, which boasts more than 800 metres of centrally heated corridors, leading to it be nicknamed the 'Death Star' after the space station in the *Star Wars* movies. The commander of British Forces South Atlantic Islands is now a tri-service, one star appointment, with officers from the three UK armed services taking turns in the chair.

The British Army now only keeps a reinforced infantry company of around 150 troops on the Falklands. It is supported by a similar number of gunners from the Royal Artillery who operate a battery of Sky Sabre surface-to-air missiles that defend the islands. During 2021 the veteran Rapier missiles were replaced with the Sky Sabre to complete the modernisation of the air defences of the Falklands. Early warning of attack is provided by a network of radar stations on the island's highest peaks operated by the RAF.

The days of the Royal Navy maintaining a frigate or destroyer in the area, supported by a nuclear-powered attack submarine, are long gone. The wars in Iraq and Afghanistan forced these expensive and scarce assets to be re-deployed elsewhere. A frigate last operated around the Falklands in 2015.

The Royal Navy now usually has a River-class patrol vessel operating in the South Atlantic in support of the ice patrol ship HMS *Protector*. The old HMS *Endurance* was scrapped in 1991 and replaced by a second hand ice breaker. The new HMS *Endurance* was replaced by the current patrol ship, another second hand ice breaker, in 2013.

Heavily armed RAF Typhoon fighter jets outclass anything in the Argentine air force. *(MOD)*

Eurofighter Typhoon	
Crew	1
Length	15.96m (52ft 4in)
Wingspan	10.95m (35ft 11in)
Max take-off weight	23,500kg (51,809lb)
Maximum speed	2,125km/h (1,320mph, 1,147kts) / Mach 2.0
Combat range	1,389km (863 miles, 750nm) Air defence with 10-minute loiter
Armament	
Guns 1 × 27 mm Mauser BK-27 revolver cannon with 150 rounds	
Air-to-air missiles	• AIM-120 AMRAAM • Meteor • ASRAAM
Air-to-ground missiles/bombs	• Brimstone guided air-to-ground missile • Storm Shadow cruise missile • Paveway II/III/Enhanced Paveway series of laser-guided bombs (LGBs) • 500-lb Paveway IV
LITENING III laser targeting pod	

HMS *Invincible* was one of two aircraft carriers deployed with the task group. *(DPL)*

ROYAL NAVY AND MERCHANT
SHIPS OF TASK FORCE

To retake the Falklands, the biggest mobilisation of naval power since World War Two was undertaken by the Royal Navy. In addition to the fighting ships of the Royal Navy, the Royal Fleet Auxiliary and Royal Maritime Auxiliary Service (RMAS) dispatched support vessels.

The Falklands task group was critically dependent on supplies and cargo carried on merchant vessels mobilised for the conflict. Known as Ships Taken up from Trade, or STUFT, they were the unsung heroes of the war. Every ship that went 'Down South' between April 2 and June 14, 1982 is listed below.

HMS *Fearless* and Royal Fleet Auxiliary vessels head south in April 1982. *(DPL)*

Type 21 frigates such as HMS *Alacrity* were the work horses of the task group. *(DPL)*

Sea Harriers were forward deployed to assault ships in San Carlos Water during June 1982 to reduce the burden on the aircraft carriers. *(DPL)*

The *Contender Bezant* carried more Chinook helicopters south but only arrived off the Falklands after the end of the conflict. *(Think Defence)*

OPERATION CORPORATE SHIPS
APRIL 2 TO JUNE 14, 1982

Royal Navy Warships				
Name/Class/Type/Pennant	Commanding Officer	Loss/Damage	Sailed South	Return to UK (1982 unless specified)
Aircraft Carriers				
HMS *Hermes* (R12)	Captain LE Middleton		April 5 from Portsmouth	Jul-21
HMS *Invincible* (R05)	Captain JJ Black		April 5 from Portsmouth	Sep-17
Landing platform docks				
HMS *Fearless* (L10)	Captain ESJ Larken		April 6 from Portsmouth	Jul-15
HMS *Intrepid* (L11)	Captain PGV Dingemans		April 26 from Portsmouth	Jul-14
Type 82 destroyer				
HMS *Bristol* (D23)	Captain A Grose		April 10 from Portsmouth	Sep-17
Type 42 destroyers				
HMS *Sheffield* (D80)	Captain JFTG Salt	Hit by Exocet 4 May, sunk May 10	April 2 from Ex Spring Train Gibraltar	
HMS *Coventry* (D118)	Captain D Hart-Dyke	Bombed and sunk May 25	April 2 from Ex Spring Train Gibraltar	
HMS *Glasgow* (D88)	Captain AP Hoddinott	Bombed May 12	April 2 from Ex Spring Train Gibraltar	Jun-18
HMS *Cardiff* (D108)	Captain MGT Harris		May 12 from Gibraltar	Jul-28
HMS *Exeter* (D89)	Captain HM Balfour		May 7 from West Indies	Jul-28
County Class Destroyers				
HMS *Antrim* (D18)	Captain BG Young	Hit by unexploded bomb May 21	April 2 from Ex Spring Train Gibraltar	Jul-17
HMS *Glamorgan* (D119)	Captain ME Barrow	Damaged by Exocet June 11	April 2 from Ex Spring Train Gibraltar	Jul-19
Type 22 frigates				
HMS *Brilliant* (F90)	Captain JF Coward		April 2 from Ex Spring Train Gibraltar	Jul-12
HMS *Broadsword* (F88)	Captain WR Canning	Hit by bomb May 25	April 8 from Ex Spring Train Gibraltar	Jul-23
Type 21 frigates				
HMS *Active* (F171)	Commander PCB Canter		May 10 from Devonport	Aug-03
HMS *Alacrity* (F174)	Commander CJS Craig		April 5 from Devonport	Jun-24
HMS *Antelope* (F170)	Commander N.J Tobin	Hit by bomb and sunk May 24	April 5 from Devonport	
HMS *Ardent* (F184)	Commander AWJ West	Hit by bomb and sunk May 21	April 19 from Devonport	
HMS *Ambuscade* (F172)	Commander PJ Mosse		April 3 from Ex Spring Train Gibraltar	Jul-07
HMS *Avenger* (F185)	Commander HM White		May 10 from Portsmouth	Sep-10
HMS *Arrow* (F173)	Commander PJ Bootherstone		April 2 from Ex Spring Train Gibraltar	Jul-07
Leander-class frigates				
HMS *Andromeda* (F57)	Captain JL Weatherall		May 10 from Devonport	Sep-10
HMS *Argonaut* (F56)	Captain CH Layman	Hit by bombs May 21	April 19 from Devonport	Jun-26
HMS *Minerva* (F45)	Commander SHG Johnston		May 10 from Devonport	Aug-03
	Commander PV Rickard		May 10 from Devonport	Sep-10
Rothesay-class frigates				
HMS *Yarmouth* (F101)	Commander AS Morton		April 8 from Ex Spring Train Gibraltar	Jul-28
HMS *Plymouth* (F126)	Captain D Pentreath	Hit by bombs June 8	April 2 from Ex Spring Train Gibraltar	Jul-14
Ice patrol ship				
HMS *Endurance* (A171)	Captain NJ Barker		Oct 13, 1981 from Portsmouth	Aug-20
Castle-class patrol vessels				
HMS *Leeds Castle* (P258)	Lieutenant-Commander CFB Hamilton		April 29 from Portsmouth	Aug-20
HMS *Dumbarton Castle* (P265)	Lieutenant Commander ND Wood		April 30 from Portsmouth	Aug-20
Churchill-class submarines				
HMS *Conqueror* (S48)	Commander CL Wreford-Brown		April 4 from Faslane	Jul-03
HMS *Courageous* (S50)	Commander RTN Best		April 4 from Faslane	Aug-13
Valiant-class submarines				
HMS *Valiant* (S102)	Commander TM Le Marchand		May 3 from Faslane	Jul-26
Swiftsure-class submarines				
HMS *Spartan* (S111)	Commander JB Taylor		April 1 from Gibraltar	Jul-24
HMS *Splendid* (S112)	Commander RC Lane-Nott		April 1 from Faslane	Jun-12
Oberon-class submarines				
HMS *Onyx* (S21)	Lieutenant-Commander AO Johnson		April 1 from unknown location	Aug-18

Royal Navy Warships				
Name/Class/Type/Pennant	Commanding Officer	Loss/Damage	Sailed South	Return to UK (1982 unless specified)
Hecla-class survey vessels				
HMS *Hecla* (A133)	Captain GL Hope		April 14 from Gibraltar	Jul-29
HMS *Herald* (A138)	Commander RIC Halliday		April 24 from Portsmouth	Jul-21
HMS *Hydra* (A144)	Commander RJ Campbell		April 24 from Portsmouth	Sep-24
Trawler/Minesweepers - Minesweeper Auxiliary (MSA) 11th MCM Squadron				
HMS *Cordella*	Lieutenant-Commander M Holloway		April 27 from Portland	Aug-11
HMS *Farnella*	Lieutenant R Bishop		April 27 from Portland	Aug-11
HMS *Junella*	Lieutenant-Commander M Rowledge		April 27 from Portland	Aug-11
HMS *Northella*	Lieutenant-Commander J Greenop		April 27 from Portland	Aug-11
HMS *Pict*	Lieutenant-Commander D Garwood		April 27 from Portland	Aug-11

Royal Fleet Auxiliary				
Tankers				
RFA *Olna* (A123)	Captain JA Bailey RFA		April 26 from Portsmouth	Sep-17
RFA *Olmeda* (A124)	Captain GP Overbury RFA		April 5 from Devonport	Jul-12
RFA *Tidespring* (A75)	Captain GW Gaffey RFA		April 2 from Ex Spring Train Gibraltar	Jul-22
RFA *Tidepool* (A76)	Captain S Redmond RFA		Sailed from Caribbean, arrive Ascension April 27	
RFA *Blue Rover* (A270)	Captain DA Reynolds RFA		April 16 from Portsmouth	Jul-17
RFA *Appleleaf* (A79)	Captain GPA McDougall RFA		April 2 from Ex Spring Train Gibraltar	Aug-09
RFA *Brambleleaf* (A81)	Captain MSJ Farley RFA		April 5 from Mombassa, Kenya	
RFA *Bayleaf* (A109)	Captain AET Hunter RFA		April 26 from Devonport	Aug-31
RFA *Plumleaf* (A78)	Captain RWM Wallace RFA		April 19 from Portland	Aug-26
RFA *Pearleaf* (A77)	Captain J McCulloch RFA		April 5 from Portsmouth	Aug-13
Landing Ship Logistic				
RFA *Sir Bedivere* (L3004)	Captain PJ McCarthy RFA	Hit by bomb May 24	April 29 from Marshwood	Nov-16
RFA *Sir Galahad* (L3005)	Captain PJG Roberts RFA	Hit by bombs May 24 and June 8, Scuttled 26 June	April 6 from Devonport	
RFA *Sir Geraint* (L3027)	Captain DE Lawrence RFA		April 6 from Devonport	Jul-23
RFA *Sir Lancelot* (L3029)	Captain CA Purcher-Wydenbruck RFA	Hit by bombs May 24	April 6 from Marchwood	Aug-18
RFA *Sir Percivale* (L3036)	Captain AF Pitt RFA		April 5 from Marchwood	Jul-23
RFA *Sir Tristram* (L3505)	Captain GR Green RFA	Hit by bombs June 8	April 2 from Belize	Jun-15
Supply ships				
RFA *Regent* (A486)	Captain J Logan RFA		April 19 from Portland	Sep-15
RFA *Resource* (A480)	Captain BA Seymour RFA		April 6 from Rosyth	Jul-19
RFA *Fort Austin* (A386)	Captain SC Dunlop RFA		April 2 from Ex Spring Train Gibraltar	Jun-28
RFA *Fort Grange* (A385)	Captain DGM Averill RFA		May 14 from Devonport	Oct-03
RFA *Stromness* (A344)	Captain JB Dickenson RFA		April 7 from Portsmouth	Jul-19
Helicopter support ships				
RFA *Engadine* (K08)	Captain DF Freeman RFA		May 10 from Devonport	Jul-30
RMAS Typhoon (A95)	Captain JN Morris RMAS		April 4 from Portland	Sep-24
RMAS *Goosander* (A94)	Captain A MacGregor RMAS		May 3 from Rosyth	Aug-11
Merchant Navy Ships Taken Up From Trade (STUFT)				
Liners				
Canberra	Captain DJ Scott-Mason		April 9 from Southampton	Jul-11
Uganda	Captain JG Clark		April 19 from Gibraltar	Aug-13
Queen Elizabeth 2	Captain P Jackson		May 12 from Southampton	Jun-11
Roll-on-Roll-off ferries				
Elk	Captain JP Morton		April 9 from Southampton	Jul-21
Baltic Ferry	Captain E Harrison		May 9 from Southampton	April 12, 1983
Europic Ferry	Captain WJC Clarke		April 25 from Portland	Jul-17
Nordic Ferry	Captain B Jenkins		May 9 from Southampton	Jul-29
Norland	Captain DA Ellerby		April 26 from Portsmouth	February 1, 1983
St Edmund	Captain MJ Stockman		May 19 from Devonport	February 28, 1983
Tor Caledonia	Captain A Scott		May 20 from Portsmouth	May 8, 1984
Container / Cargo ships				
Astronomer	Captain HS Bladen		June 8 from Devonport	Dec-03
Atlantic Conveyor	Captain IH North	Hit by Exocet May 25, sunk May 30	April 25 from Devonport	

Royal Fleet Auxiliary				
Name/Class/Type/Pennant	Commanding Officer	Loss/Damage	Sailed South	Return to UK (1982 unless specified)
Atlantic Causeway	Captain MHC Twomey		May 14 from Devonport	Jul-27
Avelona Star	Captain H Dyer		June 10 from Portsmouth	Jan 24, 1983
Contender Bezant	Captain A MacKinnon		May 21 from Devonport	Sep-23
Geestport	Captain GF Foster		May 21 from Portsmouth	Aug-18
Laertes	Captain HT Reid		June 8 from Devonport	Aug-21
Lycaon	Captain HR Lawton		May 4 from Southampton	April 21 1983
St Helena	Captain MLM Smith		June 13 from Portland	Jun-11
Saxonia	Captain H Evans		May 8 from Portsmouth	Jun-28
Tankers				
Alvega	Captain A Lazenby		May 5 from Portsmouth	March 21, 1984
Anco Charger	Captain B Hatton		April 24 from Fawley	Dec-02
Balder London	Captain KJ Wallace		May 12 from Portsmouth	Aug-15
British Avon	Captain JWM Guy		April 26 from Devonport	Jan 8, 1983
British Dart	Captain JAN Taylor		April 22 from Loch Striven	Jul-19
British Esk	Captain G Barber		April 11 from Portland	Jun-08
British Tamar	Captain WH Hare		April 14 from Milford Haven	June 20, 1983
British Tay	Captain PT Morris		April 9 from Devonport	Oct-26
British Test	Captain TA Oliphant		April 18 from Gibraltar	Jul-04
British Trent	Captain PR Walker		April 17 from Isle of Grain	Jul-05
British Wye	Captain DM Rundle		April 25 from Devonport	Jul-11
Eburna	Captain JC Beaumont		April 18 from Devonport	Jul-31
Fort Toronto	Captain RI Kinnier		April 19 from Southampton	Apr-84
GA Walker	Captain EC Metham		June 10 from Devonport	Sep-84
Scottish Eagle	Captain A Terras		May 19 from Milford Haven	October 23, 1983
Tugs / Repair / Support Ships				
British Enterprise III	Captain D Grant		May 26 from Rosyth	Aug-29
Iris	Captain A Fulton		April 29 from Southampton	Nov-30
Irishman	Captain W Allen		April 10 from Portsmouth	Oct-29
Salvageman	Captain AJ Stockwell		April 10 from Portsmouth	Jun-22
Stena Inspector	Captain D Ede		June 6 from Savannah, Georgia	November 13, 1983
Stena Seaspread	Captain N Williams		April 16 from Portsmouth	Aug-18
Wimpey Seahorse	Captain MJ Slack		May 13 from Rosyth	Sep-04
Yorkshireman	Captain P Rimmer		April 13 from Portsmouth	July 23, 1983

Tankers, such as RFA *Tidepool*, kept the task group fuelled and ready for action. *(US Navy)*

The landing ship RFA *Sir Tristram* cross decks her cargo off Ascension Island in April 1982. *(DPL)*

BRITISH AIR ORDER OF
BATTLE

 Aircraft and helicopters from all three UK armed services took part in *Operation Corporate* between April 2 and June 14, 1982

Royal Navy – Fleet Air Arm

800 Naval Air Squadron
12 Sea Harrier FRS1 air defence/ground attack aircraft (embarked on HMS *Hermes*)

801 Naval Air Squadron
Eight Sea Harrier FRS1 air defence/ground attack aircraft (embarked on HMS *Invincible*)

809 Naval Air Squadron
Eight Sea Harrier FRS1 air defence/ground attack aircraft (four subsequently absorbed into 800 Squadron and four absorbed into 801 Squadron)

820 Naval Air Squadron
11 Sea King HAS5 anti-submarine helicopters (embarked on HMS *Invincible*)

824 Naval Air Squadron
Five Sea King HAS2 support helicopters (embarked on RFA *Olmeda*, RFA *Fort Grange*)

825 Naval Air Squadron
11 Sea King HAS2 support helicopters (formed from 706 Squadron, embarked on *Queen Elizabeth 2*, and *Atlantic Causeway* and operated ashore in utility role)

826 Naval Air Squadron
Nine Sea King HAS5 anti-submarine helicopters (embarked on HMS *Hermes*)

845 Naval Air Squadron
14 Wessex HU5 support helicopters (embarked on RFA *Resource*, RFA *Fort Austin*, RFA *Tidespring*, HMS *Intrepid* and ashore at Ascension Island)

846 Naval Air Squadron
Nine Sea King HC4 support helicopters (embarked on HMS *Hermes*, HMS *Fearless*, HMS *Intrepid*, *Canberra*, *Elk*, *Norland*)

847 Naval Air Squadron
16 Wessex HU5 support helicopters (embarked on RFA *Engadine* and *Atlantic Causeway*, then ashore)

848 Naval Air Squadron
12 Wessex HU5 support helicopters (embarked on RFA *Regent*, RFA *Olna*, RFA *Olwen*, *Atlantic Conveyor*, then ashore)

815 Naval Air Squadron
19 Lynx HAS2 maritime helicopters (embarked on HMS *Alacrity*, HMS *Ambuscade*, HMS *Andromeda*, HMS *Antelope*, HMS *Ardent*, HMS *Argonaut*, HMS *Arrow*, HMS *Avenger*, HMS *Brilliant*, HMS *Broadsword*, HMS *Cardiff*, HMS *Coventry*, HMS *Exeter*, HMS *Glasgow*, HMS *Minerva*, HMS *Penelope*, HMS *Sheffield*)

815 Naval Air Squadron
10 Wasp HAS1 utility and anti-submarine helicopters (embarked on HMS *Active*, HMS *Endurance*, *Contender Brezant*, HMS *Hecla*, HMS *Herald*, HMS *Hydra*, HMS *Yarmouth*, HMS *Plymouth*)

737 Naval Air Squadron
Two Wessex HAS3 maritime helicopters (embarked on HMS *Glamorgan*, HMS *Antrim*)

Royal Marines
3 Commando Brigade Aviation Squadron RM
Nine Gazelle and six Scout utility helicopters (operated ashore)

Army Air Corps
656 Squadron AAC
Six Gazelle and six Scout utility helicopters (operated ashore)

Royal Air Force
1 (Fighter) Squadron
10 Harrier GR3 ground attack aircraft (embarked on HMS *Hermes* and at San Carlos FOB ashore)

18 (Bomber) Squadron
Eight Chinook HC1 support helicopters (embarked on *Atlantic Conveyor* and *Contender Brezant*), then ashore on Ascension Island and Falklands

Fleet Air Sea Harriers and RAF Harrier GR3s proved highly effective and robust aircraft in many roles during the Falklands War. *(DPL)*

Based at Wideawake Island, Ascension Island
(Not including transport aircraft supporting air bridge from UK)

44, 50 and 101 Squadrons
Five Vulcan B2 bombers

55 & 57 Squadron
14 Victor K2 tankers/reconnaissance aircraft

42 Squadron
Two Nimrod MR1 maritime patrol aircraft

47 Squadron
Four Hercules transport aircraft

120, 201, 206 Squadrons
Eight Nimrod MR 2P maritime patrol aircraft

Based on San Felix Island, Chile
51 Squadron
One Nimrod R1 electronic intelligence gathering aircraft

HMS *Broadsword*'s Lynx helicopter was badly damaged by an Argentine bomb. *(DPL)*

The mighty Vulcan's *Black Buck* raids were legendary and one bomb from Flight Lieutenant Martin Withers' V-Bomber stopped the Argentines using fast jets from Port Stanley airport. *(USAF)*

The Victor tanker was the key to allowing RAF bomber, maritime patrol, and transport aircraft to operate in support of the task group around the Falklands. Radar equipped Victors flew maritime reconnaissance missions ahead of the South Georgia operation. *(RuthAS)*

BRITISH ORDER OF **BATTLE**
The Battle for Port Stanley, June 14, 1982

Land Forces Falkland Islands
Commander: Major-General Jeremy Moore RM
Deputy Commander: Brigadier CJ Waters
Commander, Royal Artillery:
Colonel BT Pennicott

Command, Control and Communications
30 Signals Regiment (rear link communications)
Force Elements
Special Boat Squadron (67 men)
22 SAS Regiment (Lt Col HM Rose)
• D Squadron
• G Squadron
• 603 Tactical Air Control Party
• 264 Signals Squadron
• RAF Special Forces Detachment
Postal courier communications unit
detachment of 2 PC Regiment RE
Detachment 47 Air Despatch Squadron RCT
11 Field Squadron RE
Harrier Forward Operating Base
(FOB) at Port San Carlos

3 Commando Brigade RM
Commander: Brigadier Julian Thompson RM
Command, Control and Communications
3 Commando Brigade HQ and Signals Squadron
Y Troop RM

Infantry Manoeuvre Units
40 Commando, Royal Marines (Lt Col MPJ Hunt)
42 Commando, Royal Marines (Lt Col NF Vaux)
45 Commando, Royal Marines
(Lt Col AF Whitehead)
3rd Battalion, Parachute
Regiment (Lt Col HWR Pike)

Artillery
29 Commando Regiment RA
(Lt Col MJ Holroyd Smith, CRA)
(18 x 105mm L118 Light Guns in 7, 8, 79 Batteries)
148th (Meiktila) Battery RA (Naval Gunfire
Support Forward Observation (NGSFO)
Attached
29 Field Battery, 4 Field Regiment RA
(Six x 105mm L118 Light Guns)

Air Defence
43 Air Defence Battery RA (12 x Blowpipe)
T Battery 12 Air Defence Regiment
RA (Eight x Rapier Missile)
3 Commando Brigade Air Defence Troop
RM (12 x Blowpipe Missile launchers)

Aviation/Air Support
3 Commando Brigade Aviation Squadron RM
(Nine x Gazelle helicopters, six x Scout helicopters)
605, 611, 612 Tactical Air Control Parties RM
613 Tactical Air Control Party

Reconnaissance
3rd Troop, B Squadron, Blues and Royals (Two x
Scorpion, Two x Scimitar, One x Samson)
1 Raiding Squadron, RM (17 x Rigid Raiding Craft)
Mountain and Arctic Warfare Cadre RM

Engineer
59 Independent Commando Squadron RE
2 Troop 9 Parachute Squadron RE
Detachment 49 EOD Squadron
33 Engineer Regiment RE
RAF Bomb Disposal Team

Logistic & Medical/Brigade Administrative Area
Commando Logistics Regiment,
RM (Lt Col I Helberg)
• Medical Squadron RM (comprising Surgical
  Support Team RN) Commando Forces Band
  (stretcher-bearers, Parachute Clearing Troop)
• Commando Ordnance Company RM
• 81st Ordnance Company RAOC
• 91st Ordnance Company RAOC
• Elements Workshop Squadron REME
• Elements of 17 Port Regiment RCT
• Section 19 Field Ambulance RAMC
• 20 Postal Courier Squadron RE

5 Infantry Brigade
Commander: Brigadier Tony Wilson
Command, Control and Communications
5 Infantry Brigade Headquarters
and Signals Squadron
244 Signals Squadron (air support)
81 Intelligence Section

Infantry Manoeuvre Units
2nd Battalion, Scots Guards (Lt Col MIE Scott)
1st Battalion, Welsh Guards (Lt Col JF Rickett)
1st Battalion, 7th Duke of Edinburgh's
Own Gurkha Rifles (Lt Col D Morgan)
2nd Battalion, Parachute Regiment (Lt Col H
Jones VC, replaced by Lt Col David Chaundler)

Artillery
HQ 4 Field Regiment, RA
97 Battery Royal Artillery (Six x
105mm L118 Light Guns)

**Royal Marines board a Royal Navy Sea King
HC4 transport helicopter.** *(DPL)*

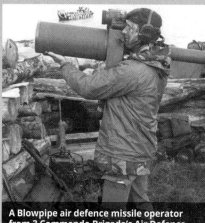

**A Blowpipe air defence missile operator
from 3 Commando Brigade's Air Defence
Troop protects San Carlos Water.** *(DPL)*

Air Defence
63 Squadron RAF Regiment (Eight x Rapier)
Troop 43 Air Defence Battery, 32 Guided
Weapons Regiment RA (Six x Blowpipe)
Troop, T Battery 12 Air Defence
Regiment RA (Four x Rapier)

Engineer
36 Engineer Regiment RE (Lt Col G Field)
• 3 Field Squadrons RE
• 50 Field Squadrons RE
• 9 Parachute Squadron RE
• 61 Field Support Squadron RE
• 1 x Field Troop, 20 Field Squadron
  RE (att 9 Para Sqn RE)

Aviation/Air Support
656 Squadron AAC (Six x Gazelle
helicopter, six x Scout helicopter)
601 Tactical Air Control Party
602 Tactical Air Control Party

Reconnaissance
4th Troop, B Squadron, Blues and Royals (Two x
Scorpion, two x Scimitar, one x Samson)

Logistic & Medical/Brigade Administrative Area
10 Field Workshop REME
81 Ordnance Company RAOC
407 Troop RCT (Snowcat vehicles)
Royal Military Police Platoon, 160
Provost Regiment, RMP
Platoon, 518 Company RPCs
16 Field Ambulance RAMC
21 Postal Courier Squadron RE

**Royal Marines collect Argentine weapons
abandoned in Port Stanley after the
surrender.** *(DPL)*

**Royal Engineers clear Argentine mines after
the conflict.** *(DPL)*

IN MEMORIAL

The Fallen of the Falklands War

BLUE BEACH MILITARY CEMETERY AT SAN CARLOS

Between April and June 1982, 255 members of the British Armed Forces made the ultimate sacrifice. Three Falkland Islanders were also killed in the war. Many of the war dead were temporarily buried in a field cemetery near San Carlos Settlement. The 174 personnel killed at sea received naval burials at sea or their remains were lost in air crashes or inside sunken warships, which were declared official war graves.

In November 1982, the remains of 64 military personnel and Hong Kong Chinese civilians were returned to the United Kingdom at the request of the families in a break from British military tradition established during World War One. Other families chose for the bodies of their loved ones to remain on the islands. The family of Victoria Cross recipient Lieutenant Colonel H Jones wanted him to remain in the soil of the islands he fought and died to liberate.

The Commonwealth War Graves Commission subsequently took over the care of the Blue Beach Military Cemetery at San Carlos and established a permanent memorial to the fallen. It contains the remains of 13 military personnel who were killed in the war and one soldier who died on the islands in 1984. The remains of two other personnel were laid to rest in individual graves at Goose Green and Port Howard.

The British Military Cemetery at San Carlos. *(Lyubomir Ivanov)*

ARGENTINE MILITARY CEMETERY

The Argentine Cemetery at Darwin. *(Tomás Terroba)*

The Argentine armed forces suffered 649 dead during the conflict. Nearly half, 323, were lost when the cruiser ARA *General Belgrano* was sunk. After British forces recaptured the Falklands in June 1982, the remains of Argentine servicemen were gathered together in temporary graves.

The British offered to return the remains of the fallen Argentine soldiers to the mainland, but the Junta declined, saying they had already been laid to rest in their homeland. A dedicated cemetery was completed by the British military authorities near Darwin in December 1982 and the fallen Argentine soldiers were buried with full military honours. The remains of three Argentine pilots in remote locations were later discovered and buried in the cemetery.

More than 100 fallen Argentine soldiers out of 236 in the Darwin cemetery were not immediately identified after the conflict. In 2017 the International Committee of the Red Cross (ICRC) began a project to use DNA technology to identify the remains of Argentine soldiers in the Darwin cemetery and by early 2021 had identified 121 of them.